Everyday Sel Educators

If you're an educator experiencing burnout, compassion fatigue, or vicarious trauma, this book will help you embrace tangible self-care practices to improve your well-being both in and out of the classroom. Using the framework of the "window of capacity" – the zone of the nervous system arousal in which a person is able to function most effectively – the authors illustrate not only "the why" of self-care, but also "the how." Chapters explore how stress at school impacts personal life, the way teacher self-care benefits students, and ways in which schools can implement and support well-being. The book includes a variety of tips and interactive activities to help you identify your own needs and implement helpful practices. You'll leave with a toolbox of information and simple practices to effectively advocate for your well-being in educational spaces and beyond.

Carla Tantillo Philibert is a recognized expert on Social-Emotional Learning (SEL), mindfulness, and yoga practices in the school setting. She is the founder of Mindful Practices, co-founder of Class Catalyst, and oversees a team of dedicated practitioners who have served thousands of students and teachers across the country since 2006.

Chris Soto has worked in both private and public educational settings in a variety of roles, always with the goal of expanding emotional and mental health supports for students. Currently, he is the Social-Emotional and Mental Health Coordinator for Durham Public Schools and an Instructor at the University of Pennsylvania Graduate School of Education.

Lara Veon, LCPC, is a holistic body-inclusive psychotherapist, trauma consultant, educator, and yoga teacher. She currently works in private practice in the Chicago area where she specializes in the treatment of trauma and consults with schools across the nation on SEL and trauma-informed practices.

Also Available from Carla Tantillo Philibert
(www.routledge.com/k-12)

Everyday SEL in Early Childhood:
Integrating Social-Emotional Learning and Mindfulness into
Your Classroom

Everyday SEL in Elementary School:
Integrating Social-Emotional Learning and Mindfulness into
Your Classroom

Everyday SEL in Middle School:
Integrating Social-Emotional Learning and Mindfulness into
Your Classroom

Everyday SEL in High School:
Integrating Social-Emotional Learning and Mindfulness into
Your Classroom

Everyday Self-Care for Educators

Tools and Strategies for Well-Being

Carla Tantillo Philibert, Chris Soto, and
Lara Veon

Routledge
Taylor & Francis Group

NEW YORK AND LONDON

First published 2020
by Routledge
52 Vanderbilt Avenue, New York, NY 10017

and by Routledge
2 Park Square, Milton Park, Abingdon, Oxon, OX14 4RN

Routledge is an imprint of the Taylor & Francis Group, an informa business

Library of Congress Cataloging-in-Publication Data
Names: Tantillo Philibert, Carla, author. | Soto, Chris, author. | Veon, Lara, author.
Title: Everyday self-care for educators : tools and strategies for well-being / Carla Tantillo-Philibert, Chris Soto, Lara Veon.
Description: New York : Routledge, 2019. | Includes bibliographical references.
Identifiers: LCCN 2019007878 (print) | ISBN 9780367229795 (hbk) | ISBN 9780367229825 (pbk) | ISBN 9780429277818 (ebk)
Subjects: LCSH: Teachers–Job stress. | Teachers–Mental health. | Teachers–Health and hygiene. | Teaching–Psychological aspects. | Stress management. | Well-being.
Classification: LCC LB2840.2 .T36 2019 (print) | LCC LB2840.2 (ebook) | DDC 371.1–dc23
LC record available at https://lccn.loc.gov/2019007878
LC ebook record available at https://lccn.loc.gov/2019980342

ISBN: 978-0-367-22979-5 (hbk)
ISBN: 978-0-367-22982-5 (pbk)
ISBN: 978-0-429-27781-8 (ebk)

Typeset in Palatino
by Swales & Willis, Exeter, Devon, UK

Contents

Activities vii

Meet the Authors ix

1 **Introduction** 1

2 **Stress at Home and School** 27

3 **The Impact of Teacher Self-Care on Students** 59

4 **Implementation and Support for Well-Being** 71

Conclusion 81

References 91

Activities

Are You Experiencing Compassion Fatigue? 28

Body Scan 31

Holistic Self-Care Wheel Assessment. 34

Balanced Breath 37

Yoga Sequences. 38

The "No Zone" (or "Hard Stop") for Schoolwork at Home . . . 43

The Jar of Gratitude 44

The Inner Compass (a daily intention practice) 45

Well-Being Ally and Action Plan 47

Sensory Experiences. 49

Be the Tree. 63

Climb the Mountain. 64

Breathe in the Breeze 74

Breathe in the Sun 74

Memory Minute 88

Owning My Story Journal 88

One Word Check-in/Check-out 89

Drawing Out Loud 89

Meet the Authors

Carla Tantillo Philibert is a recognized expert on Social-Emotional Learning (SEL), mindfulness, and yoga practices in the school setting. She is the founder of Mindful Practices, co-founder of Class Catalyst, and oversees a team of dedicated practitioners who have served thousands of students and teachers across the country since 2006. Carla has a master's degree in curriculum and instruction and is a certified yoga teacher. She is a regular, featured speaker at CEC, NSBA, NAESP, and the Kripalu Yoga in School Symposium. She is the author of *Cooling Down Your Classroom: Using Yoga, Relaxation and Breathing Strategies to Help Students Learn to Keep Their Cool* and the Everyday SEL series of K–12 books (Routledge 2016). Carla lives with her husband and two children in Chicago, Illinois.

Dr Chris Soto's career has focused on the intersection of education and emotional wellness. He has worked in both private and public educational settings in a variety of roles, always with the goal of expanding emotional and mental health supports for students. Recently, his attention has turned to advocating for systemic strategies to support the well-being of teachers, who deserve far more from our society than they receive. Currently, Chris is the Social-Emotional and Mental Health Coordinator for Durham Public Schools and an Instructor at the University of Pennsylvania Graduate School of Education. He lives with his wife, two sons, and dog in Hillsborough, North Carolina.

Lara Veon, LCPC, E-RYT 200 is a holistic body-inclusive psychotherapist, trauma consultant, educator, and yoga teacher. For two decades, Lara has worked in schools as a teacher, learning specialist, and most recently as a director of counseling. She currently works in private practice in the Chicago area where she specializes in the treatment of trauma and consults with schools across the nation on SEL and trauma-informed practices.

1

Introduction

Walking through the halls of stressed school communities as a mental health professional can lead to heartfelt and challenging interactions with educators. Too many times to count, a teacher or administrator has jokingly asked "Can I get counseling, too?" with a dark undercurrent of truth to the question. Sometimes, on occasions when we have enough time and space to respond with full authenticity, these moments can result in tearful conversations about the stressful nature of working in schools. Opening up the topic of stress and well-being with educators is like drinking from a fire hydrant – once the spigot is opened a flood often ensues.

While our work in education, therapy, and counseling has primarily been with children and adolescents, we have had the growing sense for many years that focusing on counseling children, though imperative, is like putting a Band-Aid on a broken leg. Evidence from neuropsychology and education is mounting that the affective systems of teachers and students are tangled together throughout the school day and that focusing exclusively on direct support for children will yield disappointing results.

That is because, like all humans, the brains of teachers and students are wired to share emotional experiences with one another. We are a social species, and learning is inherently a social act. Therefore, it is vital for us to have the capacity to read and respond to each other's affective cues and to model them. This process – which is a foundational component of human development – takes place through mirror neurons, which fire when we are imitating behaviors to learn new skills. This is a vital part of the learning experience in formal classrooms, which are designed to produce this effect. Students are cued, under optimal conditions, to follow the lead of their teachers through reciprocal imitations (Zhou, 2012). In other words, emotions are contagious by design.

Emotions in Schools

There are few places where this contagion effect is more evident than in schools, where emotions – both positive and negative – can spread like brush fires. The educational researcher Andy Hargreaves (2001) refers to schools as *emotional geographies*, which he defines as "the patterns of spatial and experiential distances that help shape, configure, and color the feelings and emotions about ourselves, our world, and each other" (p. 106). Students are physically close to one another every day for long periods of time, and so these patterns exert themselves recursively throughout the school day. Anyone who has spent significant time in the classrooms and hallways of a brick and mortar school will recognize how quickly anger, fear, excitement, or laughter can spread across the building.

Under ideal conditions, this is a good thing. Strong learning communities are rich with *achievement emotions*, such as interest and enjoyment (Pekrun, Frenzel, Goetz, & Perry, 2007). Learning is a social act with social purposes, and so the spread of these positive emotions can create and amplify opportunities for all children in a school.

This effect is also true for negative emotions, however. Students who experience unhealthy levels of family or community conflict, for example, without the developmental assets to learn coping skills to manage these experiences will manifest fear, mistrust, and anger in the classrooms and hallways of their school. Because of the contagious nature of emotion, other members of the school community will also experience the repercussions of these experiences, an effect called *vicarious traumatization.*

While the affective-behavioral manifestations of traumatic experience are at the severe end of the continuum, this effect is not exclusive to extreme circumstances. As Hargreaves points out, every school interaction is laced with an emotional valence. Therefore, the entire school is subject to this transfer of feeling states. Ideally, the shared emotional understanding is a learning-directed encounter between an adult and a child, like the excitement of a new idea or the congratulatory feeling of a good grade on a test. This effect, where two or more people experience a shared emotional understanding, has been referred to by Walter Denzin as *emotional intersubjectivity* (2007). Most effective teachers have the capacity to sync with their students' emotions in this way by offering activities and regulatory strategies to help them stay in the sweet zone of learning.

Positive or negative, large or small, there is no doubt that emotions reverberate across campuses. Like a stone being thrown into a lake, the ripples are largest that are closest to the stone. It is doubtful, for example, that mild anger or anxiety in an art class will be felt in the main office unless accompanied by a troubling behavior. To that point, the "size" of the emotion matters, as well. Large rocks make large ripples, while pebbles make ripples that can scarcely be seen spreading. Less extreme emotions are less likely to spread, while strong emotions (positive or negative) are quite likely to impact those in close proximity.

The Emotional Labor of Teaching

Teachers are particularly subject to the contagion effect. And while more severe behaviors are more likely to impact teachers more severely, they can also experience vicarious manifestations even in mild or generally positive cultures because teachers work in close proximity all day, nearly every day, to children whose regulatory capacity has not fully developed! Like math or reading, it takes time and experience for them to learn effective strategies to manage their emotions. My three-year-old son, for example, literally fell on the floor crying this morning because I asked him to put on socks. While older children and adolescents certainly have more advanced skills than that, the emotional pendulum does swing wide for many years before they develop the social-emotional competencies to modulate and moderate affect-based behaviors.

It is impossible for teachers to avoid being impacted by those emotions. In fact, it is an *implicit part of their job description.* Take a second to think about our cultural stereotypes of teachers and the role expectations that they carry: We *expect* our teachers to care for their students and we frown on educators who do not exhibit the patient and optimistic behaviors that we would demand, given the nature of their profession. We romanticize self-sacrifice and expect our teachers (understandably) to be emotionally invested in the well-being and success of every one of their students.

That being the case, teachers have a high bar every day regarding their emotional regulatory capacity. At a minimum, they are required to put away their negative feelings in the service of forming and maintaining quality learning relationships with their students. But not only are they asked to be in close proximity with small under-regulated humans, they are also expected to utilize all available pedagogical and interpersonal skills to infect them with feelings of motivation, and even inspiration. As such, emotional regulation is central, not peripheral, to the teaching experience. In fact, it is a fiduciary job requirement that is often overlooked by school leaders as a foundational *and teachable* skill set.

The responsibility to apply social-emotional competency as a part of their job description has been described by educational researchers as *emotional labor*. Originally described by Arlie Hochschild in her book *The Managed Heart* (1983), emotional labor is the management of feelings to create bodily displays in accord with organizational norms and enacted for institutional goals – usually profit. Early work on emotional labor focused on customer service occupations, such as flight attendants and restaurant servers, in which workers interact intermittently but consistently with consumers. During those interactions, they are required to both amplify positive and suppress negative emotions. The motto "service with a smile" is the prototypical example of emotional labor. Teachers enact emotional labor, then, when they are not feeling excited but act as if they are as they greet children at the beginning of the school day, or when they stuff away their frustration at student misbehavior in order to model the virtue of patience. In other words, any time a teacher up-regulates or down-regulates an emotion to serve the institutional goal of learning, it is a form of emotional labor.

In and of itself, this is not a good or a bad thing. Teachers are drawn into the field precisely because they receive tangible psychological benefits from the role, often in the form of enhanced self-esteem (Isenbarger & Zembylas, 2006). Most teachers perform caring tasks willingly and reap some measure of reward from maintaining the identity of a caring professional. For all of the stresses of teaching, it is an honorable career that is authentically democratic and invariably optimistic.

Sadly, this optimistic sensibility can compound stressors when unmet academic standards, disruptive student behavior, and limited resources create a wide gap between the archetype and the reality. This can be especially true for new teachers and teachers in high need communities. The subjective experience of this gap can lead to micro-interactional dilemmas, because teachers may be forced to choose many times every day between sharing their real feelings of disappointment or frustration and self-regulating towards a demeanor that is congruent with their professional expectations. Most teachers choose appropriately, of course, by working to psychologically vacuum pack inappropriate responses to challenging situations. When this incongruence reaches intolerable levels, however, they can be faced with feelings of in-authenticity and dissonance (Oplatka, 2009). This incongruence, discussed at some length below, can result in physical, psychological, and behavioral manifestations of stress that impact not only the teacher, but also their classroom and school community.

Teacher Stress as an Indicator of a National Concern

The implications of this truth are far reaching. There is a growing body of literature that emphasizes the negative consequences of large scale cognitive and emotional dissonance – a pattern that has contributed to an epidemic of teacher burnout and turnover, particularly in high poverty schools.

While not every teacher is suffering, many are. In 2017, "Teachers reported having poor mental health for 11 or more days per month at twice the rate of the general U.S. workforce. They also reported lower-than-recommended levels of health outcomes and sleep per night" (Educator Quality of Life Survey, 2017, p. i). Based on a Gallup poll, Greenberg, Brown, and Abenavoli (2016) note that "46% of teachers report high daily stress, tied with nurses for the highest among all occupations" (p. 2). The toxic national discourse on education has compounded teacher worry, with nearly half of the teachers in a national survey reporting that their stress has increased significantly as a result of "the national political environment" (Rogers, 2017, p. 3). As a result of these factors, job satisfaction in the teaching profession is at an all-time low (Metlife, 2013).

There is a sense of unease that national reports of teacher stress may be a canary in the coal mine regarding public education. Teachers are at the heart of the very mission of public schools – providing a social and economic safety net for our democratic institutions through access to quality learning opportunities. That so many of them report high levels of stress and low levels of satisfaction should precipitate both data-informed reflections on the most common symptoms and research-based approaches towards the most effective solutions.

The remainder of this chapter, then, will emphasize the importance of awareness and self-advocacy in light of these distressing trends. To jumpstart that approach, we will describe key research on two of these symptoms, *high teacher turnover* and *low student achievement*, which educational research has identified as indicators of unhealthy levels of teacher stress where they occur. In doing so, we draw a link between the national picture and the micro-experience of teachers, who experience stress as the neurological, physiological, and psychological manifestation of a low-control, high-stress career.

The purpose of this work is not to discourage, but rather to find avenues towards wellness through validating the true teaching experience, providing them with tools and strategies to have essential conversations with school leadership as we begin to think through practical solutions to a problem that is both local and national. As a solution, we present the growing consensus that mindfulness-based professional development can help teachers improve their social-emotional competence and their capacity to regulate emotions in the service of forming and maintaining relationships with the children they serve.

Starting a Self-Advocacy Toolbox

One of the goals of our book is to give educators a toolbox of information and simple practices to effectively advocate for their well-being. Stigmas associated with mental health can be a barrier to address emotional well-being at work, and employees often hide anxiety and depression for fear of professional repercussions. A large U.K. study, for example, found that 86% of the British workforce would hesitate to approach a colleague about a perceived mental health concern, and 35% did not approach anyone for help the last time they experienced a significant mental health issue (Deloitte Center for Health Solutions, 2017). Feeling comfortable to have essential conversations about stress with supervisors, in particular, is an important step towards self-care, especially when its manifestations may be impacting job performance. According to a 2017 report, however, only 36% of employees believe that they could rely on the support of their supervisor if things get difficult (Hellebuyck, Nguyen, Halphern, Fritze, & Kennedy, 2017).[1]

Having conversations about stress and wellness can be very challenging for teachers. First, they are responsible for the well-being of children and may be disinclined to share perceived vulnerability with school administrators for fear that misconstrued or exaggerated concerns could impact their employment. In general, teachers have not traditionally wielded sufficient institutional power to self-advocate with confidence.

These conversations are also constrained by the structure of schools and the policies required to operate them. Broad responsibility for adult supervision at all times makes it a logistical challenge to block out enough time to unpack stress, which can be a messy topic (recall the fire hydrant analogy). For some of the same reasons, policies are often in place that make it difficult to practice self-care, such as human resource policies that make clear distinctions between sick days and personal days or school-based policies that treat Monday and Friday teacher absences punitively. More abstractly, the topic can be difficult to address because of the misperception that summers off are a luxurious perk, and that the mental health benefits of this perk extend across the entire school year like some kind of time release medication. Finally, the ever-present cultural assumption of archetypal self-sacrifice infuses the prospect of caregiver guilt when teachers do assert their right to self-care opportunities.

The conversation can also be challenging for school administrators, who are responsible for fully ensuring competent adult supervision and instruction at all times, particularly given the significant drop-off in substitute performance (through no fault of the substitutes, themselves). It can be hard for administrators to have conversations about social-emotional competence without extremely high levels of interpersonal competence, themselves, especially when they are dealing with significant stressors, themselves.

There is also an implicit barrier to the style of feedback that administrators are used to giving. In our consultations with school Principals, we have found that those who are ready and able to give highly effective instructional feedback are often quite hesitant to address performance related concerns about mood, demeanor, or emotional expression. This makes some sense if you consider the difference between how you might perceive a supervisory suggestion that you need organizational coaching and a suggestion that you need to work on your expressive demeanor. In other words, it is difficult to give and receive effective feedback in the social-emotional domain because it can feel personal rather than technical.

These are the exact conversations that must happen, however, for the sake of all of the stakeholders in a school's ecology. First, it is vital to recognize that stress has clear and identifiable symptoms that often take the form of unproductive workplace behaviors (McLean & Connor, 2015). These symptoms impact the culture of the classroom and the learning of individual students, most often by harming the learning connection between student and teacher, discussed more at length below. In that way, stress does ultimately lead to impaired job performance. Too often, however, behavioral issues that surface as a result of chronic stress are treated *exclusively* as performance issues rather than as manifestations of stress that can be mitigated with stress reduction strategies (Hughes, 2001). Focusing exclusively on instructional techniques with a low-performing teacher who exhibits symptoms, for example, is not likely to yield desired improvements in performance because the unhealthy behaviors are both a cause and a result of the stress and are thus likely to continue in the absence of treating the root concern.[2] When a teacher struggles to keep her emotions together because of job-related stressors, then, it is a necessary conversation to have – in the best interests of the teacher, the administrator, and the children.

Research shows that the consequences of unaddressed stress operate across all levels of our educational ecology, from the micro, such as individual student achievement, to the macro, such as national policy conversations about educational equity. Because the stakes are so high, we have to be able to see both the forest *and* the trees. As you are reading, then, we hope that you will consider how to present this information to colleagues and supervisors in a way that will advance a call for teacher wellness, both locally and nationally.

The Individual Impact of Stress on Teachers

In this section, we address both the individual impact of stress (the trees) and highlight the broader implications (the forest) for public education and school success. Before we start talking about the negative elements of stress, however, it is important to note that worry is not bad, in and of itself. When we experience small, manageable doses of stress or anxiety we become motivated to alter our behavior. If a student is not worried about her performance on a test then she is unlikely to study for it. Ideally, anxiety serves an important function.

Similarly, work-related stressors can carry important performance-related information and lead to effective professional development when managed effectively. Although there has been a significant amount of pushback on the now ubiquitous reliance of public education on standardized testing, for example, there is little doubt that teachers generally work hard to improve their instructional practices as a result of those scores (although the argument rages about *which* instructional practices are improved, and to what end).

Conversely, too *much* stress, or stress that is unaddressed or occurs without functional control mechanisms, like mindfulness tools, has negative implications. On an individual level, it has tangible, health-related consequences that are biological, psychological, and relational. Our nervous systems place a high value on creating alarms that echo throughout the body when we experience subjective distress. These alarms precipitate chemical (and neurological) responses that are often long-lasting. Because of their responsibility for the well-being of children, and depending on context, teachers can spend a good portion of their day on high alert, making them subject to these chemical responses. Some of these responses are discussed in more detail in Chapter 2.

The important piece to recognize for this conversation is that the lived experience of stress is not just "in our heads." Instead, it has concrete, physiological components that intersect with the psychological well-being and job-related behaviors of teachers who are experiencing it. Bellingrath, Weigl, and Kudielka (2009), for example, found that teachers who report high levels of stress also have high levels of Allostatic Load (AL), which is found by measuring the ten biological factors commonly associated with stress (like cortisol, blood-pressure, norepinephrine, etc.). AL can be conceptualized as the physiological measure of the "burden exacted on the body through attempts to meet life's demands" (p. 37), which can serve as a measure of job-related stress.

This same research also found that AL was higher in teachers who perceived a greater imbalance between the work that they put into teaching and the rewards that they received as a result. Termed *effort-reward imbalance* (ERI), the gap between our expectations of work and our reality of work predicts higher levels of *emotional exhaustion*, one of the three primary components of *burnout*. The larger the gap, the more likely we are to experience the thoughts and feelings associated with emotional exhaustion (e.g. lack of energy, feeling stuck or trapped). Burnout, which is chronic stress that occurs as a result of working directly with people (Schwarzer & Hallum, 2008), is a serious concern for teachers, particularly those in high need schools (discussed below). In addition to *emotional exhaustion*, teachers suffering from burnout would also experience some combination of *reduced job-related self-efficacy* and *student depersonalization* (Berryhill, Linney, & Fromewick, 2009).

Educational researchers are focusing an increasing amount of attention on these components of teacher burnout, and also some ways of countering them. Failing to address high levels of stress in the workplace generally has two outcomes, both undesirable. The first is turnover, which occurs when a teacher exits a school, a district, or the teaching profession entirely. The second – and perhaps even more toxic – occurs when teachers who are stressed stay in the classroom because of financial or identity considerations and continue to teach with the behavioral manifestations of unmanaged burnout.

It is important to note that high stress levels are not easy to tolerate. Understandably, people will seek some kind of resolution to feelings of exhaustion or ineffectiveness. Depending on job market fluctuations, professional qualifications, and personal considerations, however, it may be quite difficult to change jobs or careers.

The chances of attempting a change are significantly higher, though, for those teachers who are suffering. Once stress becomes unmanageable, then a teacher has a difficult choice to make (either consciously or unconsciously); that is, she can stay in her current position and increase her effort, or she can leave for another school or district. If she leaves, she might also choose to leave the profession, taking her acquired experience and skills with her.

The Problem of Teachers Leaving

Unfortunately, more and more teachers are making the choice to leave the field. Survey data over the past several decades shows that teacher attrition has been increasing steadily since the 1990s and that this attrition accounts for nearly 90% of the demand for new teachers.

Teacher surveys are shedding an uncomfortable light on this shift. While salary is one component of teacher attrition, dissatisfaction (not retirement) accounts for at least 55% of teacher turnover (Carver-Thomas & Darling-Hammond, 2017). Teachers report that discipline issues and localized administrative concerns top the list of reasons for that dissatisfaction, suggesting that the increasing levels of teacher turnover is not an "inexorable demographic trend" that are coming as a result of changes in the overall workforce (Ingersoll, 2004, p. 4); Rather, it is coming because of an enormous increase in systemic pressures on teachers that are occurring at the same time as their role is being politically and professionally devalued. If we keep in mind our previous discussion about the high value that teachers place on affirmations and support, combined with the information about the costs of effort-reward imbalance, then it is easy to see how a teacher who is experiencing emotional exhaustion without expected benefits would opt to try her luck elsewhere.

The Problem of Teachers Staying Despite Burnout

While teacher turnover is a problem of national significance, it is not the only option available to the teacher who struggles with unmanaged stress; she also has the option to stay in the classroom in spite of her struggles. As it relates to school quality, this might actually be the more concerning choice, because teachers who stay in the classroom tend to negatively impact the culture and climate of their school by distancing themselves from their students and/or their craft. In fact, they often lower their academic expectations in order to reduce the gap between their ideal and their lived experience (Ronfeldt, Lankford, Loeb, & Wyckoff, 2013).

Indeed, research by Hughes (2001) found that underneath the alarming data on teachers who turn over is another group of teachers (ranging from 30% to 60%) who would prefer not to continue but feel trapped because of life situations (finances, age, retirement, fear, etc.). This conundrum is challenging for a teacher who begins to experience emotional exhaustion and attempts to recalibrate her professional identity; she can either reduce her effort in order to decrease her anxiety, or increase her job responsibility in hope of increasing her rewards. If she does the former, then her job performance will likely decrease and raise her anxiety about the prospect of job loss. If she chooses the latter – but her efforts are thwarted by low student performance or lack of administrative support – then her frustration will increase along with her emotional exhaustion.

Without supportive interventions, teachers who continue under these circumstances will likely experience the most insidious component of burnout, the *depersonalization* of their students. Depersonalization, "refers to feelings of cognitive distance, indifference, or cynicism" towards the students, who are the primary recipients of teachers' efforts (Arens & Morin, 2016, p. 800). Depersonalization is often tied to emotional exhaustion, because teachers who suffer from burnout simply do not have the energy to examine the feelings underneath challenging student behaviors and are thus more likely to be excessively punitive in their responses, even during relatively mild interactions (Jennings & Greenberg, 2009). Teachers who generally carry with them an angry or impatient demeanor are likely to damage connections with their students. And because teachers are the holders of the academic content in traditional educational settings, students *require* interpersonal connection with them for formal learning to occur.

It is through this broken connection that teacher emotional exhaustion and student depersonalization take their toll, often resulting in *lowered academic achievement*. Teachers who have difficulty maintaining functional learning connections with their students because they convey an overly frustrated, anxious, or depressed demeanor have a hard time teaching them effectively. McLean and Connor (2015), for example, found that teachers who exhibited more symptoms of depression were "less likely to maintain high quality learning environments," and that students in their classrooms scored lower on standardized math tests than peers at the same skill level with teachers who did not report symptoms. In this study, the effect was particularly significant for students with low math skills. Math is a particularly scaffolded subject, with one level building on the next, and so teachers who are not interpersonally accessible for students cement and compound their previously existing skill deficits.

The effect is not exclusive to math, however. Arens and Morin (2016) also found a strong relationship between emotional exhaustion, depersonalization, and poor student outcomes, but for standardized scores in English and Writing. Furthermore, students with depressed teachers may become disengaged because emotional contagion literally depresses the room. Oberle and Schonert-Reichl (2016), for example, found that students who spend time in the morning with teachers who exhibit symptoms of burnout have significantly higher levels of stress-related cortisol in their own blood than students who spend the morning with teachers who do not.

The Antidotes: Social-Emotional Competence and Positive Relationships

Thankfully, the converse is also true for teachers who exude excitement, interpersonal warmth, and a generally positive demeanor. Positive emotional experience forms the basis of how students perceive support in the classroom, so approachable teachers who create a culture of emotional safety, belonging, and enjoyment (including laughter) are more likely to gain access to students' academic pathways. Indeed, Arens and Morin (2016) found that students who feel greater support from their teachers do better in school. Frenzel, Goetz, Ludtke, Pekrun, and Sutton (2009) also found that greater teacher enthusiasm produces greater student enjoyment, which positively impacts academic achievement. In essence, teachers who show a respect for the subjective experience of students and who are at least moderately enjoyable to spend time around are also more likely to gain students' prolonged attention regarding academic matters.

The mediating variable between teacher stress and student outcomes, therefore, seems to be student-teacher connection. This is not a new finding, but one that has been building evidence for quite some time. Developing children are thirsty for adult connection, even if they do not show it (especially during the transitional years of middle school). It takes an adult who is mindfully aware of their own biases and assumptions to display the non-judgmental attitudes and behaviors that students require for those connections to occur.

This authentic non-judgment – complete with the social-emotional competencies that are needed to keep that non-judgmental demeanor in the face of challenging behaviors – can be exceptionally difficult to maintain for teachers who may be experiencing low energy or high stress. This is especially true for teachers who already lack the cognitive or emotional skills to engage and motivate their students (Klusmann, Kunter, Trautwein, Ludtke, & Baumert, 2008). While this is true for all teachers, burnout concerns are even more acute for those who have a low frustration tolerance, strong authoritarian beliefs, or who are highly self-critical (Bernard, 2016). These teachers are generally less likely to maintain the interpersonal flexibility to stay engaged with students during times of high stress (particularly students who might challenge their self-beliefs) to the point that academic content cannot be accessed. Teacher stress is most toxic, then, when it damages existing social-emotional competencies because academic performance suffers when students cannot or will not connect with them.

It is important to note that in strong learning communities, educators do not have to rely on pre-existing social-emotional competencies. SEC can be also built through professional development opportunities that focus on interpersonal skill-building. Unfortunately, high stress schools too often shy away from committing sufficient resources towards these opportunities because they are more complicated to implement and monitor (than instructional PDs) and generally viewed as peripheral to the essential function of schools.

A Note on Equity

We hope that we have made it clear that unmitigated stress can impact teachers who work in even the mildest of school settings because of the nature of the role, which is interpersonally dense. It is important to emphasize, however, that schools in high stress communities are substantially more likely than their counterparts to experience the systemic consequences of stress – high turnover and low academic achievement. Teachers who work in high need schools have the same role demands, but the emotions and behaviors that they encounter are often on the severe end of the continuum due to the embodied stress that students bring into the school building with them.

Students of color are disproportionately impacted by this reality. Indeed, Carver-Thomas and Darling-Hammond's extensive research on the impact of stress on turnover found that "turnover rates are 70% higher for teachers in schools serving the largest concentrations of students of color" (2017, p. 3). Not only that, but teachers who leave are particularly challenging to replace because of recruitment barriers associated with serving low-income and minority students. So while it costs around $4,000 to replace rural teachers, it typically costs from $17,000 to $20,000 to recruit, develop, and train every teacher who exits an urban school. For a variety of reasons, however, schools continue to focus on recruitment efforts rather than retention efforts – a strategy that does not typically yield positive results for either school climate or achievement (Ingersoll, 2004).

The reasons for the uninspired results of recruitment steer us back to the impact of relationships in learning. When teachers encounter and become saturated by the manifestations of community stress without an outlet, they are more likely to leave. And because turnover is far more likely in high-need schools, interpersonal continuity is annually disrupted between students, teachers, and parents in the low income communities that usually surround them. When we add this piece to what we have already discussed regarding the impact of relationships on academic achievement, we can surmise that high turnover amplifies developmental and resource deficits in communities where the vital links to learning opportunities are often frayed or broken. In this way, the cumulative stress does more than just impact teachers; it also contributes to a cycle of underperformance and the long-term destabilization of schools for those children with the most need, making teacher stress an equity issue with national significance.

Working towards Solutions

Teacher burnout, then, can be conceptualized as a cycle. At the teacher level, unsustainable dissonance is created when outcomes (rewards) are not commensurate with inputs (effort) or when expectations are not aligned with reality. This results in emotional exhaustion and contributes to low job-related self-efficacy, the depersonalization of students, and ultimately disengagement. This disengagement takes the form of teachers who exit the profession, move to a different school, or stay in their own school with significantly reduced performance and a depressed or toxic demeanor. All of these outcomes have negative implications for student engagement and achievement. Furthermore, the shared stress of high stakes testing feeds the cycle by pressurizing instruction at the expense of solutions that build the social-emotional competencies that support learning connections.

It is not enough for teachers, school administration, and district administration to be aware of this cycle. To effectively address it, they need to collaborate on when and how to intervene in the cycle in order to stabilize and reverse it, starting with proactive approaches that build social-emotional competencies and help to emotionally vaccinate teachers from the predictable stressors that they face.

In their research on the impact of teacher stress and how to address it, Greenberg et al. (2016) found three approaches that schools and school systems can take to mitigate the negative impacts of stress and produce positive outcomes: *organizational interventions*, like increased salary, a participatory work environment, and job restructuring, are designed to prevent high levels of stress from occurring; *organizational/individual interface interventions*, such as mentoring programs, wellness programs, and social-emotional learning programs, focus on skill-building and social support; and *individual interventions*, for instance mindfulness and stress management programs, focus exclusively on skills and strategies that help teachers cope internally with stressors through mindfulness and cognitive reframing techniques.

All three approaches can be effective depending on context. In the private sector, for example, there is an increasing focus on broad wellness programming with a focus on improving employee productivity. Giant tech companies like Google and Apple, as well as numerous Fortune 500 companies, have developed an important understanding that inspired employees are more productive employees than those who are simply satisfied to have a job (Vozza, 2017). Thus, they consciously show commitment to their workers by providing them access to health, wellness, and quality of life resources ranging from flex work schedules to on site exercise equipment. Although schools usually lack the financial resources to provide in-kind benefits, awareness of the value of such programs has started to trickle down to the educational sector, where a quick scan of the internet reveals numerous mindfulness-related stress management programs targeted towards teachers. While a discussion about how to select programs is beyond the scope of this book, it is clear that every institution should begin with a thorough needs assessment in consultation with relevant stakeholders before large scale implementation. It does not help either the employees or the bottom line for companies to invest in canned programs that do not specific to context because they will simply not be used.

Education is a good example of the need for programmatic specificity. As discussed above, schools have a unique responsibility to provide adult supervision and student instruction at all times. It is a part of the job description of teachers and administrators, which they accept when they pursue and take a position in their chosen field. These scheduling needs place unique constraints and affordances on traditional schools as they balance and integrate systems that meet the needs of their students with those that meet the needs of their staff.

Partly for this reason, the following two chapters focus on individual mindfulness interventions and practices that can be folded into the everyday work of teaching before turning to a discussion about system-wide approaches. Schools and school systems may have large scale processes that provide benefits, content, or structures that pave the way for well-being, but at the end of the day the thoughts and behaviors that give us satisfaction are enacted individually. Through the chapters that follow, then, we provide tools and strategies for educators who would like to improve their capacity to regulate stress and consciously work towards experiencing the compassion, enjoyment, and gratitude that should ideally be a part of our work every day with children. As importantly, we seek to provide readers with ways to frame mindfulness that will help them advocate for both district-wide systems and school-based practices.

The Argument for Mindfulness in Schools

The use of mindfulness-based approaches to address these concerns has been growing. Mindfulness has been defined simply as "Paying attention, on purpose, in the present moment, non-judgmentally" (Kabat-Zinn, 1994, p. 2). The process of developing mindful habits is neurologically akin to developing physical skill sets that build muscle memory, like riding a bike or playing the guitar, and building cognitive schemas, like improving math skills or connecting narrative themes across literary genres. This is more than just an analogy, because practicing acute and sustained awareness over time builds neural connections that fundamentally alter networks in the brain in the same way as developing those skills (Roeser, 2014). Practicing mindfulness is not, therefore, a "soft skill," but a concrete mechanism to improve focus.

Improving mindfulness is important for teachers because it allows them to exert more effortful control over their own thoughts, emotions, and behaviors. Because negative thoughts can lead to distressing emotions, and because distressing emotions can lead to unproductive or disruptive behaviors, improving control in these domains can improve the chances that a teacher will make thoughtful and strategic choices when students are misbehaving or underperforming. Indeed, a thorough meta-analysis on the impact of Mindfulness-Based Interventions (MBIs) found their broad positive impact on both the well-being and performance of educators to be "encouraging" (Lomas, Medina, Ivtzan, Rupprecht, & Eiroa-Orosa, 2017, p. 139).

Jennings and Greenberg (2009) suggest that the primary mediating variable between mindfulness training and teacher well-being and job performance is SEC. As discussed above, unmanaged stress leaves teachers emotionally exhausted and significantly less likely to exert the efforts necessary to form and maintain positive learning relationships. It also makes them more likely to have negative reactions to challenging situations, thus creating a "self-sustaining cycle of disruption" (p. 492). Jennings and her colleagues found that teachers trained in mindfulness techniques raised their ability to emotionally adapt to challenging situations and lowered their psychological distress, as well as their time urgency (Jennings et al., 2017). Harris, Jennings, Katz, Abenavoli, and Greenberg (2015) found that mindfulness training increased positive affect, improved classroom management, and decreased distress tolerance. And Kemeny et al. (2012) found that a 42-hour course on meditation and emotional regulation course actually increased teachers' level of compassion towards their students.

In this way, the effective practice of mindfulness functions both to prevent and heal the symptoms of stress. It serves a preventative function by allowing teachers to maintain their own regulatory capacity even in the face of challenging behaviors, thus minimizing the severity of conflict when it occurs. It also serves a healing function by allowing the autonomic system to more thoroughly reset when stress does occur. For this reason, we view the conscious development of mindfulness-based practices in schools as the solution that is both the most practical and the most powerful of the interventions to educator stress.

A Story from the Field

Maurice R. Swinney Chief Equity Officer, Chicago Public Schools

I've heard self-care, wellness, and well-being throughout my 12 years as a high school administrator. Take care of yourself is what people say.

For many people of color, self-care may show up differently.

Self-care for me is releasing myself from feeling like I have to live up to whiteness.

Being successful at wellness during my 12+ years as high school administrator, as an African American man, a black man, living in white dominated culture proved more difficult than one might think. There were pressures – a series of undue burdens – to be a black man who represents all things black. Whether pressed upon me or self-imposed, room for vulnerability or opportunities to make mistakes were minimal. I wanted to always do my best work because I knew that students would benefit, reminding myself that the temporary anguish is worthy of the outcome. But I also knew that longevity would only occur if I created space to acknowledge my moods, my thoughts, and wonderings.

Over time, wellness became the thing I had to gift myself to continue to serve my school community, specifically my students. I had to rescue my mind through music, writing, and vacations. I learned that finding and playing a song to shine light on my moods allowed someone else's words to speak for me. I started to take quick weekend trips to cities where my friends like to be refueled; they affirmed me as I learned to continuously affirm myself. Sitting on the floor meditating, rolling my neck, released the tension that in my neck and shoulders. I found ways to release the emotional tax that I carried when I was misunderstood across race.

Painting a bleak picture about the struggles of being a leader of color is not my intention; noting that people of color struggle for self-care uniquely because there are additional stressors that can stifle their work in service to both students of color and white students. A part of self-care is the avoidance of over-reliance from white people to deal with students of color. White administrators have to been like the alchemist to meet the needs of students of color; they must get better at serving students (and adults) across racial lines in the same way that we would expect that cis-men and women seek to understand the marginalizing experiences of our LGBTQ+ communities. Those who have the most power and influence have to step into the complexity of relating to people of color, so that they can grow, too.

Wellness is a collectivist approach to ensuring that the community is well. The community must thrive because if one is not well, maybe none of us are.

Notes

1. Notably, the same report found that recognition and praise are significantly more important to employees than compensation.
2. This would not be true, of course, if the teachers' stress originated from a lack of confidence due to a limited range of instructional strategies.

2

Stress at Home and School

According to data from the National Survey of Children's Health, roughly half of the students under 18 years of age attending school in our nation's classrooms have experienced at least one adverse childhood experience (ACE) (Johns Hopkins Bloomberg School of Public Health), such as the death or incarceration of a parent, witnessing or being a victim of violence, or living with someone who has been suicidal or had a drug or alcohol problem. Factor in exposure to community violence or food insecurity, which are not formally considered ACEs, and the number climbs even higher. Then add students who have additional needs due to learning challenges, illness, or mental health issues and the number of young people experiencing acute, chronic, or traumatic stress skyrockets.

As we know, the impact of this is not isolated to only our students. Those who educate them are at risk of experiencing compassion fatigue, sometimes also referred to as vicarious trauma or secondary trauma. Compassion fatigue is the cumulative effect of stress resulting from caring for and helping traumatized or suffering people (Figley, 1995). Empathic distress, another term coined by Zen teacher and medical anthropologist, Roshi Joan Halifax, describes a trauma-like state that can occur through empathizing deeply with a situation over which one has no control. According to Halifax, those experiencing empathic distress can be pushed to "edge states" like pathological altruism or vital exhaustion (burnout) where they become depleted to the point of physical or mental self-harm through engaging in care of others (Halifax, 2018). While there is variance in the definitions of these terms in the research, we propose for the sake of this text that there is a spectrum of toxic stress experienced by today's educators, and that spectrum includes these varying states of vital exhaustion and heartbreaking distress that can adversely impact their functioning in daily life.

Recovery from these states begins first with awareness. Review the checklist of symptoms below, placing an "X" underneath "Rarely," "Sometimes," or "Often" if it speaks to your experience.

Activity: Are You Experiencing Compassion Fatigue?

Are you experiencing:	Rarely	Sometimes	Often
Anger/cynicism			
Fear			
Guilt			
Hopelessness			
Anxiety			
Exhaustion			
Sense of hopelessness			
Living in a state of hypervigilance			
Feeling unsafe/anticipating danger			
Difficulty embracing complexity/ tendency towards concrete thinking			
Difficulty listening			
Loss of creativity			
Poor self-care			

Sleeping/eating disturbances
Increased illness
Reduced productivity
Difficulty focusing
Withdrawal from social activities
Increased substance use
A loss of connection and trust in your systems of
    meaning
Denial

(National Child Welfare Workforce Institute)

Stress: What's Going On in My Brain and Body

We know what happens to trigger stress in an educational environment: large classrooms, high needs, a dearth of resources, demanding schedules, and that tiny clause that so many contracts include that reads "… and whatever other duties are deemed necessary." When the stress response in the brain is activated, there is an automatic, instantaneous, and instinctive process that happens in the brain that is important to understand. Knowledge of this process can help us better understand why chronic stress can cause a reaction that is similar physiologically to a post-traumatic response. Here is a simplified explanation:

The Amygdala, the brain's "fear system" or "fire alarm" is activated by a stressor or perceived stressor. Once it sounds an alert to the brain that there is a threat (regardless of whether there actually *is* a real life-threatening threat), a stress response becomes initiated in the body in which the body moves into survival mode. This is what we mean when we use the phrase "fight/flight/freeze." The freeze response occurs when fighting or fleeing is not possible.

When the stress response is initiated, and we move into fight/flight/freeze, chemicals such as norepinephrine, and "stress hormones" such as adrenaline and cortisol release into the bloodstream in order for us to survive. If too much of these are produced acutely over and over or chronically maintained in the body at high levels, it can be harmful to all systems in the body and potentially cause the symptoms outlined above. All the body's resources are going to survival and, as a result, it can be difficult to have any left over for relating, thinking, and learning.

Small Changes Become Big Transformation: The Path to Recovery

Questions often asked when discussing compassion fatigue are "Are we too far gone? Knowing our realities in schools today, how can we ever hope to recover? Please, what do we do NOW?" The good news is that recovery *is* possible! While brains can become wired as a result of a chronic stress response, the process known as neuroplasticity refers to the ability of the human brain to change as a result of one's experience. The network of neurons created by chronic stress and vicarious trauma *can* change with repetition and practice. Much like the transition from caterpillar to chrysalis to butterfly, this change happens gradually through awareness, self-assessment, mindfulness, body wisdom, and both formal and informal holistic practices – all of which are designed to bring one back into a state of balance in order to live lives full of connection and foster a sense of well-being.

Mindful Awareness and Body Wisdom:
It Starts with Presence

These approaches are tools that intervene at the level of the nervous system to help regulate, balance mood, and improve the problematic symptoms of compassion fatigue. Many of these tools help cultivate the ability to remain in the present moment, to notice and tolerate inner experience, and to develop a new trusting relationship with one's body. Using body-inclusive approaches also provides an opportunity to restore the interpersonal and intrapersonal rhythms that are disturbed and become out of sync in chronic stress, as well as respond effectively to emotions or arousal states in the body. As psychiatrist and trauma expert, Bessel van der Kolk, says, "To feel what you feel and know what you know in your body, can go a long way toward healing" (van der Kolk, 2014).

Activity: Body Scan

The "Why": This activity builds a self-awareness practice by inviting you to be in the present moment and sense and feel your body, so you can respond effectively to its needs and care for yourself.

Supplies: Just you and your body, a chair, or floor

Script: In this experience, we will explore different sensations in the body. Rather than thinking about the body, we will directly feel and experience our body. Try to be patient with yourself, keeping as still as possible and refraining from judging what you feel. The objective is to invite curiosity and awareness without the need to label our experience. Lastly, be gentle and kind to yourself. (Note: This exercise can be done in a comfortable seated position or even a chair.)

Begin by detaching from your outer world and shifting your awareness to your body. We invite you to listen to your body. You are always in control of your practice and may come out of it at any time.

If it is comfortable, perhaps you might close your eyes. If it is not, feel free to lower your gaze to an unmoving point in the room.

As you are ready, with compassionate curiosity, begin to notice any areas of tension in your body. Notice any areas that feel relaxed. Without needing to do anything with these feelings, simply notice them.

Now bring awareness to your body seated wherever you're seated by feeling the weight of your body on the chair or the floor.

If it is accessible, begin to notice air coming in your body and leaving it.

You may deepen your breath if it is comfortable to do so.

As you inhale, notice air comes into the body. As you exhale, notice how it leaves the body.

Invite awareness of your feet on the floor. Notice any sensations in the toes, the inner arch of your feet, and the heels. Are your feet heavy? Is there a pressure or temperature you notice?

When you're ready, bring awareness now to your legs against the chair or floor. Notice where you might feel heaviness or pressure. Perhaps you might notice a lightness.

Remember, there is no wrong way to experience this.

Bring awareness to your back against the chair. Scanning from the top of the spine down to the base, focus on any areas of tension you notice. Shift to noticing where on your back you are free of tension.

Continuing with compassionate curiosity, bring your attention into your stomach area. If your stomach is tense or tight, perhaps you might let it soften. Take a breath as you are ready.

Notice your hands. Can you feel tension or tightness? Perhaps allow them to soften.

Bring awareness to your arms. Do you notice sensations? Notice higher in your shoulders. If they are tense, perhaps let them relax if it is comfortable.

Notice your neck and throat. Bring awareness to any areas of tension or the absence of tension.

Focus on your jaw. Is it tight or soft? Is your tongue at the roof of the mouth? If so, perhaps allow it to drop away. Notice your face and facial muscles. With a breath, if it feels good, allow those muscles in your face and jaw to soften.

Now notice your whole body present here in this moment. Be aware of your whole body as much as is comfortable. If you can, perhaps inhale a breath. And then exhale.

When you're ready, you can open your eyes and gently come back to the room by noticing and labeling (to yourself) three items you see in the space.

How To Story

Regina learned this body scan in a stress reduction seminar. She asked a friend with a pleasing voice to record the script on her phone. Then Regina committed to practicing the body scan each evening before bed.

The above script is adapted from Jon Kabat-Zinn's Mindfulness-Based Stress Reduction (MBSR) body scan.

Self Assessing One's Self-Care

Identifying areas of need in self-care behaviors is imperative for building the practice of mindful self-awareness and developing healthy habits that impact one's physical and mental health in positive ways. We have provided two different resources for assessing your self-care needs.

The Mindful Self-Care Scale (MSCS) is validated and standardized for determining the variety and frequency of self-care strategies (Cook-Cottone, 2015).

The Holistic Self-Care Wheel Assessment, adapted from Mary Jo Barrett's (2011) work on compassion fatigue, is modeled after the Substance Abuse and Mental Health Services Administration's (SAMHSA) Eight Dimensions of Wellness.

Activity: Holistic Self-Care Wheel Assessment

Holistic Wellness Wheel

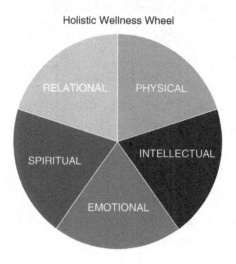

Adapted from Mary Jo Barrett, MSW

The "Why": In spite of wishful thinking, humans have a limited supply of energetic resources. Assessing both the energy expenditures and replenishers in the holistic areas of wellness allows one to prioritize needs for optimal well-being to live a balanced life.

Supplies: The holistic self-care wheel, paper, pen/pencil

Steps:

1. On a piece of paper, create a list of energy expenditures for each category on the holistic wheel. For example, on the list for "Physical," a new mom might indicate middle of the night wakings for the baby as an energy expenditure.
2. On another piece of paper, create a list of energy replenishers for each category on the holistic wheel. For example, on the list for "relational," someone might indicate a weekly group that meets around a hobby.

3. Look at both lists to determine which areas have the fewest replenishers and most expenditures. These will be your priorities on which to focus for a self-care plan.

How To Story

Jim's school was beginning to talk about self-care, and he had no idea how to assess his needs. He simply knew he felt entirely overwhelmed. Being able to frame his wellness in these six different categories and consider what in his life was expending energy and what was replenishing it helped him feel like he finally had a map towards getting help.

Additional Self-Assessment Resources

Self-care Assessment:
www.mentoring.org/new-site/wp-content/uploads/2015/09/MARCH_2015_Self_Care_Assessment.pdf
Saakvitne, K. W., & Pearlman, L. A. (1996)

Professional Quality of Life Scale:
https://proqol.org/uploads/ProQOL_5_English.pdf
www.compassionfatigue.org/pages/selftest.html

From Missing in Action to Mindfulness in Action: Formal and Informal Practices for Self-Care

Much like mindfulness, self-care can take the form of formal and informal practices. Formal practices are planned and take time out of the day, are structured and repetitive. Informal practices of self-care have roots in mindfulness meditation and consist of the ability to be fully present and "pay attention, on purpose in the present moment without judgment" (Kabat-Zinn, 1990). These practices are infused into activities we do all day every day in our lives. Both formal and informal self-care practices are aligned with holistic areas of wellness: physical, intellectual, emotional, spiritual, and relational/community. The practices below are merely a taste of the limitless supply of activities we have available to us. Often, we are engaging in the informal practices already but are not fully present. Inviting presence through awareness can shift a mindless activity to a mindful opportunity.

Formal Practices for Self-Care and Well-Being: Physical Practices

Activity: Balanced Breath

The "Why": Breathing where the length of the inhale and exhale are even initiates your nervous system relaxation response and releases hormones and chemicals in your brain, which has a calming impact on your whole system.

Supplies: Just yourself

Steps:

1. Begin seated with your feet on the ground.
2. Bring awareness to your breathing. Notice breath is coming in your body and out.
3. Now, begin to make your inhalation and exhalation the same length. Inhale to a count of 1-2-3-4 and exhale 1-2-3-4.
4. Repeat this 4-count for three rounds.
5. Now, increase the breath count to 5. Inhale 1-2-3-4-5 and exhale 1-2-3-4-5.
6. Repeat this 5-count for three rounds.
7. Next, increase the breath count to 6. Inhale 1-2-3-4-5-6 and exhale 1-2-3-4-5-6.
8. Repeat this 6-count for three rounds.
9. Releasing a focus on counts, take a full, deep breath into your body and exhale it out strongly, noticing how you feel in your body.

How To Story

Rashid is moving all day long with his 4th grade class and sometimes feels overwhelmed with their needs. He is rarely able to find quiet or be alone. He learned this breathing technique and started practicing it during bathroom breaks a couple times a day. He realized he needed these time outs and felt calmer after.

Activity: Yoga Sequences

The "Why": Yoga connects the mind and body through breath and movement. These mindful movements in the body help us stay in a present moment experience, provide relief from stress and pain, and can even enhance the quality of our sleep. Seated yoga sequences allow for a restorative practice from the comfort of our chairs while standing sequences invite the entire body into the practice.

Supplies: None required

Seated Poses: Seated Arms Stretch, Seated Twist, Gentle Neck Stretch

Seated Arms Stretch

Steps:

1. Remember yoga is not about doing poses perfectly! Simply try your best with non-judgment and listen to your body.
2. First, begin seated with your feet flat on the floor.
3. Then, raise your arms above your head and interlace your fingers.
4. Next, flip your palms to the ceiling and move your shoulders down and away from your ears.
5. Now, close your eyes, and take five deep breaths.
6. Last, if you want to take your arms over to the right and left to stretch the side body, you are invited to do so while taking five deep breaths on each side.
7. Slowly lower your arms and notice any sensations in your body.

Seated Twist

Steps:

1. First, inhale and lengthen your spine. Close your eyes and take in a deep breath. Take a moment to scan the body and

mind. Notice if there is anything negative you would like to release. With a deep exhalation, release it now.

2. Then, keeping your feet planted firmly on the ground, exhale and rotate your torso to the right side. Guide your eyes to a spot over your right shoulder on which to focus. Take five deep breaths. On the last breath, come back to center.

3. Next, still keeping your feet firmly planted on the ground, inhale and lengthen your spine. Exhale and rotate your torso to the left side. Guide your eyes to a spot over your left shoulder on which to focus. Take five deep breaths. On the last breath, come back to center.

4. Last, close your eyes and allow yourself to take five deep breaths. Just notice the pattern of breath moving in and out of your body. There is no need to change the breath; just notice it and flow with it. Bring awareness to any sensations in your body.

Gentle Neck Stretch

Steps:

1. First, inhale and lengthen your spine. Close your eyes and take a deep breath.

2. Then, sitting erect, lengthen your spine and place your left hand on your lap or the surface in front of you. Bring your right fingertips to your right shoulder.

3. Next, rotate your right elbow, so it is in line with your shoulder. With an inhalation, tilt your left ear toward your left shoulder. Maintain a still upper body while you use your right fingertips to apply light downward pressure on the right shoulder.

4. Now, take five deep breaths while maintaining a comfortable stretch in the neck. When you are done, bring yourself back to a neutral position. Roll shoulders back three times.

5. Repeating on the other side, continuing to sit erect, lengthen your spine and place your right hand on your lap or the surface in front of you. Bring your left fingertips to your left shoulder.

6. Next, rotate your left elbow, so it is in line with your shoulder. With an inhalation, tilt your right ear towards your right shoulder. Maintain a still upper body while you use your left fingertips to apply light downward pressure on the left shoulder.

7. Last, take five deep breaths while maintaining a comfortable stretch in the neck. When you are done, bring yourself back to a neutral position. Roll shoulders back three times. Notice sensations in your body.

Standing Poses: Mountain Pose, Standing Side Stretch, Tree Pose

Mountain Pose

Steps:

1. First, place your feet parallel like train tracks, plant your feet into the ground.

2. Then, extend the crown of your head to the ceiling and lengthen your spine. Roll your shoulders back as your eyes find a focal point on which to focus.

3. Now, allow your arms to draw straight down the sides of your body. Your palms can face outward or towards your body.

4. Last, distribute your weight evenly between both feet, and stand tall. Take five deep breaths.

Standing Side Stretch

Steps:

1. First, begin in mountain pose.

2. Then, raise your arms above your head and interlace your fingers.

3. Next, flip your palms to the sky and move your shoulders down and away from your ears.

4. Now, close your eyes, and take five deep breaths.

5. Then, keep your hands interlaced, feet grounded, and move your arms to the right. Take five deep breaths as you stretch the side body. Move back to neutral.
6. Now, keep your hands interlaced, feet grounded, and move your arms to the left. Take five deep breaths as you stretch the side body. Move back to neutral.
7. Slowly lower your arms, take five deep breaths, and notice any sensations in your body.

Tree Pose

Steps:

1. First, begin in mountain pose and focus your gaze on a point in front of you.
2. Then, shift your weight onto your right leg. Lift your left leg, and turn it out to the side while you keep your hips facing forward.
3. Next, place your left foot above or below the right knee (not on the knee joint). Press your foot into your leg as your leg presses back into your foot.
4. Last, lift your arms overhead like the branches of a tree. Stay as long as you'd like before bringing your left leg down to stand back in mountain pose. Take five deep breaths.
5. Repeating on the other side, shift your weight onto your left leg. Lift your right leg, and turn it out to the side while you keep your hips facing forward.
6. Next, place your right foot above or below the left knee (not on the knee joint). Press your foot into your leg as your leg presses back into your foot.
7. Last, lift your arms overhead like the branches of a tree. Stay as long as you'd like before bringing your right leg down to stand back in mountain pose. Take five deep breaths and notice any sensations in your body.

How To Story

Middle school teacher, Liza, was having a hard time understanding how adding one more thing – even if it was mindful movement – to her schedule could help her stress level. She just didn't have time!

The physical education teacher convinced her to try these sequences before her class started and again at lunch time. Liza practiced the sequences and noticed she had a few favorites that she began to do throughout the day. She even began to have her class practice together!

Intellectual Practice

> ### Activity: The "No Zone" (or "Hard Stop") for Schoolwork at Home

The "Why": Creating boundaries around how much time at home is devoted to school-related tasks can provide the brain and heart rest from the stressors of work. This can positively impact the nervous system, as well as provide time for other activities and connections that contribute to well-being.

Supplies: Calendar

Steps:

1. On the evening before you start the work week, look at your calendar, so you have a week's view of your commitments.
2. Identify the two evenings you will bring work home.
3. On your schedule, indicate "HARD STOP" at the desired time.
4. After that "HARD STOP" time, indicate the "NO ZONE" for schoolwork at home.
5. Lastly, indicate the "NO ZONE" on the other work days of the week.

> ### How To Story
>
> *Steven has been overwhelmed and often brings home his lessons plans and work to grade since his grading periods at school are frequently consumed with meetings or students wanting to talk. Often this work can absorb his evenings and impact his ability to spend time with his family. He has felt tired and disconnected, and the work he has been doing was not the quality he wanted it to be. With the help of his supervisor, he created a schedule where he only allowed himself to bring work home twice a week and on those evenings, he had a hard stop at 8pm. While it took time to adjust – mostly because of a self-imposed pressure – he began to see his relationships at home improve and noticed he slept better.*

Emotional Practice

Activity: The Jar of Gratitude

The "Why": According to the psychologist, Robert Emmons, practicing gratitude has been shown to have a positive impact on physical health, psychological well-being and our relationship with others. Gratitude contributes to positive emotions, lessons negativity, builds resilience, and improves self-worth (Emmons, 2010).

Supplies: Large mason jar (a decorative box can work too), sticky-note-sized paper, favorite marker(s)

Steps:

1. First, if you are the creative type, decorate a large mason jar with a sign titled, "Jar of Gratitude."
2. Next, every evening before going to sleep, reflect on one thing for which you are grateful (it can be anything).
3. Then, take a deep breath and notice the sensation in your body when you think about it.
4. Last, write it down on a slip of paper and put it in the jar.

* You can look at the slips at the end of each week, month or anytime you need a reminder of the positive.

How To Story

Lillian teaches third grade and it happens to be one of those years when she has 27 students and over half of them have an individualized learning plan. More often than not, she feels whatever she does, it isn't helping kids learn. Her best friend mentioned her negative attitude, and so she started the jar of gratitude as a way of bringing more positivity into her life. After a couple of weeks of this practice, Lillian's negativity has decreased. She has enjoyed the practice so much she started a "family gratitude jar." Each night before bed, her partner and children get in on the goodness, too!

Spiritual/Wisdom Practice

Activity: The Inner Compass (a daily intention practice)

The "Why": So often when our days are filled with stressful situations, it can feel like life is happening to us without anything being within our control. A daily intention practice can become an energetic "true north": a point of grounding rooted in a choice you have made from the deepest truth of your heart. It sets the tone and can become something you return to over and over throughout the day.

Supplies: Journal and pen

Steps:

1. Each morning after waking, pause for a moment and take a deep breath. Ask yourself, "what in the deepest part of my heart do I wish to have in my life today?"
2. Continuing to take deep, cleansing breaths, reflect on the answer that comes up for you.
3. When you have an answer, reframe it as if it is already happening. For example, if your answer is patience and peace it may become, "I am patient and at peace today."
4. Write your intention in your journal.

How To Story

High school teacher Darren was reluctant to believe in the power of a daily intention. He doubted one word would make all the other things that stressed him out better, and he was a bit worried about adding another item on his "to do" list. In a sense, he was right. Those stressors remained. What he found, however, was that having the morning ritual was soothing, and the ability to come back to his intention throughout the day helped him calm down when he started to feel overwhelmed.

* The Inner Compass is easily modified to a dedication practice. Instead of a personal intention, you might bring to mind a person who might need some compassion (this is a **great** practice if you're having trouble with a student and have noticed your compassion and patience waning).

Relational/Community Practice

Activity: Well-Being Ally and Action Plan

The "Why": We need allies because we simply can't do it alone. Having quality social relationships positively impacts our sense of well-being. When we are depleted or having trouble taking care of ourselves, having a well-being ally can keep us accountable, lend support, and give us access to an objective perspective, which is extremely important when we're not thinking clearly!

Supplies: A friend, family member or colleague who is willing to support your well-being

Steps:

1. When you find your ally, arrange a regular time to check in. Begin with a check-in once each week.
2. Take a self-care assessment to determine areas where you are low in resources. (See self-assessment resources.)
3. For each of those areas, create an action plan of how you can become more resourced.
4. Share the plan with your ally.
5. During the check-in sessions, review what you did to follow through on your action plan.
6. Each week, assess your needs in each area and revise your action plan.

How To Story

Kaye asked her older sister, Linda, to be her well-being ally. Linda doesn't work in education but has been concerned about Kaye's level of burnout lately. Every Sunday, the family meets for dinner at their parents' house, and the sisters agreed to take 20 minutes at the beginning of each gathering to review the plan Kaye had for the week and revise for the upcoming. Kaye has appreciated the regular check in and finds it is harder to ignore the action plan when she knows Linda will hold her accountable come Sunday.

Informal Practices: Full Sensory Experiences

Activity: Sensory Experiences

The "Why": Every moment brings with it an opportunity to have a full sensory experience. When we cultivate the ability to notice the senses in the moment without needing to change anything, we are learning to "listen" with our whole bodies, a skill that allows us to build awareness and better respond to our holistic needs.

Supplies: Just you

Steps:

1. Bring your awareness to the task you are doing.
2. Notice what you can smell.
3. Now focus on what you can see. Describe what you see to yourself.
4. Notice if there is anything you can taste.
5. Can you feel something tactile in this task? Spend a few moments exploring it.
6. Bring awareness to what you can hear while doing the task.
7. Lastly, is there a feeling you have while doing this task. Where in your body do you feel this?
8. Finish the task, and if you find your awareness drawn to something else, gently come back to the senses. This might happen over and over. That is why it is called a practice.

Some daily activities that can invite present moment awareness include the following:

◆ Showering
◆ Doing the dishes
◆ Cooking
◆ Eating
◆ Conversing
◆ Driving
◆ Standing in line

- ◆ Yard work
- ◆ Cleaning
- ◆ Playing with children
- ◆ Walking the dog
- ◆ Hugging
- ◆ Grading
- ◆ Grocery shopping

How To Story

Reggie started incorporating present moment awareness into his days after he had a panic attack during a faculty meeting. As a way to reduce stress, his doctor suggested mindfulness practices. Reggie noticed when he started, it was extremely difficult to be present in each task. His mind constantly wandered to his students or something that had happened during the day. Sometimes, it was in a loop worrying about the future. He began practicing sensory mindfulness when he was showering and doing the dishes only. Then he naturally began noticing more in other tasks. One day, he felt the familiar pounding of his heart when he was in a conflict at school, and he started to pay attention to his surroundings with his senses. It helped calm him down enough to resolve the problem.

Mindful Self-Care Scale (MSCS)

Mindful Self-Care Scale – Clinical

Source: Cook-Cottone, C. P. (2015). *Mindfulness and yoga for embodied self-regulation: A primer for mental health professionals.* New York, NY: Springer Publishing. (See text for a detailed description of the measure.)

The Mindful Self-Care Scale – Clinical is an 84-item scale that measures the self-reported frequency of behaviors that measure self-care behavior.

Self-care is defined as the daily process of being aware of and attending to one's basic physiological and emotional needs including the shaping of one's daily routine, relationships, and environment as needed to promote self-care. Mindful self-care addresses self-care and adds the component of mindful awareness.

Mindful self-care is seen as the foundational work required for physical and emotional well-being. Self-care is associated with positive physical health, emotional well-being, and mental health. Steady and intentional practice of mindful self-care is seen as protective by preventing the onset of mental health symptoms, job/school burnout, and improving work and school productivity.

This scale is intended to help individuals identify areas of strength and weakness in mindful self-care behavior as well as assess interventions that serve to improve self-care. The scale addresses 10 domains of self-care: nutrition/hydration, exercise, soothing strategies, self-awareness/mindfulness, rest, relationships, physical and medical practices, environmental factors, self-compassion, and spiritual practices. There are also three general items assessing the individual's general or more global practices of self-care.

Contact information: Catherine Cook-Cottone, Ph.D. at cpcook@buffalo.edu

*Circle the number that reflects the frequency of your behavior
(how much or how often) within past week (7 days):*

Never (0 days)	Rarely (1 day)	Sometimes (2 to 3 days)	Often (4 to 5 days)	Regularly (6 to 7 days)
1	2	3	4	5

Reverse-Scored:

Never (0 days)	Rarely (1 day)	Sometimes (2 to 3 days)	Often (4 to 5 days)	Regularly (6 to 7 days)
5	4	3	2	1

The questions on the scale follow:

Nutrition/Hydration (NH) – 7 items

I drank at least 6 to 8 cups of water	1	2	3	4	5
Even though my stomach felt full enough, I kept eating *reverse scored*	5	4	3	2	1
I adjusted my water intake when I needed to (e.g., for exercise, hot weather)	1	2	3	4	5
I skipped a meal *reverse scored*	5	4	3	2	1
I ate breakfast, lunch, dinner, and, when needed, snacks	1	2	3	4	5
I ate a variety of nutritious foods (e.g., vegetables, protein, fruits, and grains)	1	2	3	4	5
I planned my meals and snacks	1	2	3	4	5

Total _____

Average for Subscale = Total/# of items _____

Exercise (E) – 7 items

I exercised at least 30 to 60 minutes	1	2	3	4	5
I took part in sports, dance or other scheduled physical activities (e.g., sports teams, dance classes)	1	2	3	4	5
I did sedentary activities instead of exercising (e.g., watched tv, worked on the computer) *reverse scored*	5	4	3	2	1

I sat for periods of longer than 60-minutes at a time *reverse scored*	5	4	3	2	1
I did fun physical activities (e.g., danced, played active games, jumped in leaves)	1	2	3	4	5
I exercised in excess (e.g., when I was tired, sleep deprived, or risking stress/injury) *reverse scored*	5	4	3	2	1
I planned/scheduled my exercise for the day	1	2	3	4	5

Total _____

Average for Subscale = Total/# of items _____

Self-Soothing (S) – 13 items

I used deep breathing to relax	1	2	3	4	5
I did not know how to relax *reverse scored*	5	4	3	2	1
I thought about calming things (e.g., nature, happy memories)	1	2	3	4	5
When I got stressed, I stayed stressed for hours (i.e., I couldn't calm down) *reverse scored*	5	4	3	2	1
I did something physical to help me relax (e.g., taking a bath, yoga, going for a walk)	1	2	3	4	5
I did something intellectual (using my mind) to help me relax (e.g., read a book, wrote)	1	2	3	4	5
I did something interpersonal to relax (e.g., connected with friends)	1	2	3	4	5
I did something creative to relax (e.g., drew, played instrument, wrote creatively, sang, organized)	1	2	3	4	5
I listened to relax (e.g., to music, a podcast, radio show, rainforest sounds)	1	2	3	4	5
I sought out images to relax (e.g., art, film, window shopping, nature)	1	2	3	4	5
I sought out smells to relax (lotions, nature, candles/incense, smells of baking)	1	2	3	4	5
I sought out tactile or touch-based experiences to relax (e.g., petting an animal, cuddling a soft blanket, floated in a pool, put on comfy clothes)	1	2	3	4	5
I prioritized activities that help me relax	1	2	3	4	5

Total _____

Average for Subscale = Total/# of items _____

Self-Awareness/Mindfulness (SA) – 10 items

I had a calm awareness of my thoughts	1	2	3	4	5
I had a calm awareness of my feelings	1	2	3	4	5
I had a calm awareness of my body	1	2	3	4	5
I carefully selected which of my thoughts and feelings I used to guide my actions	1	2	3	4	5
I meditated in some form (e.g., sitting meditation, walking meditation, prayer)	1	2	3	4	5
I practiced mindful eating (i.e., paid attention to the taste and texture of the food, ate without distraction)	1	2	3	4	5
I practiced yoga or another mind/body practice (e.g., Tae Kwon Do, Tai Chi)	1	2	3	4	5
I tracked/recorded my self-care practices (e.g., journaling, used an app, kept a calendar)	1	2	3	4	5
I planned/scheduled meditation and/or a mindful practice for the day (e.g., yoga, walking meditation, prayer)	1	2	3	4	5
I took time to acknowledge the things for which I am grateful	1	2	3	4	5
Total					
Average for Subscale = Total/# of items					

Rest (R) – 7 items

I got enough sleep to feel rested and restored when I woke up	1	2	3	4	5
I planned restful/rejuvenating breaks throughout the day	1	2	3	4	5
I rested when I needed to (e.g., when not feeling well, after a long work out or effort)	1	2	3	4	5
I took planned breaks from school or work	1	2	3	4	5
I planned/scheduled pleasant activities that were not work or school related	1	2	3	4	5
I took time away from electronics (e.g., turned off phone and other devices)	1	2	3	4	5
I made time in my schedule for enough sleep	1	2	3	4	5
Total					
Average for Subscale = Total/# of items					

Relationships (RR) – 7 items

I spent time with people who are good to me (e.g., support, encourage, and believe in me)	1	2	3	4	5
I scheduled/planned time to be with people who are special to me	1	2	3	4	5
I felt supported by people in my life	1	2	3	4	5
I felt confident that people in my life would respect my choice if I said "no"	1	2	3	4	5
I knew that, if I needed to, I could stand up for myself in my relationships	1	2	3	4	5
I made time for people who sustain and support me	1	2	3	4	5
I felt that I had someone who would listen to me if I became upset (e.g., friend, counselor, group)	1	2	3	4	5

Total _____

Average for Subscale = Total/# of items _____

Physical/Medical (PM) – 8 items

I engaged in medical care to prevent/treat illness and disease (e.g., attended doctor's visits, took prescribed medications/vitamins, was up to date on screenings/immunizations, followed doctor recommendations)	1	2	3	4	5
I engaged in dental care to prevent/treat illness and disease (e.g., dental visits, tooth brushing, flossing)	1	2	3	4	5
I took/did recreational drugs *reverse scored*	5	4	3	2	1
I did _not_ drink alcohol	1	2	3	4	5
I practiced overall cleanliness and hygiene	1	2	3	4	5
I accessed the medical/dental care I needed	1	2	3	4	5
I did not smoke	1	2	3	4	5
I did not drink alcohol in excess (i.e., more than 1 to 2 drinks [*1 drink = 12 ounces beer, 5 ounces wine, or 1.5 ounces liquor*])	1	2	3	4	5

Total _____

Average for Subscale = Total/# of items _____

Environmental Factors (EF) – 9 items

I maintained a manageable schedule	1	2	3	4	5
I avoided taking on too many requests or demands	1	2	3	4	5
I maintained a comforting and pleasing living environment	1	2	3	4	5
I kept my work/schoolwork area organized to support my work/school tasks	1	2	3	4	5
I maintained balance between the demands of others and what is important to me	1	2	3	4	5
Physical barriers to daily functioning were addressed (e.g., needed supplies for home and work were secured, light bulbs were replaced and functioning)	1	2	3	4	5
I made sure I wore suitable clothing for the weather (e.g., umbrella in the rain, boots in the snow, warm coat in winter)	1	2	3	4	5
I did things to make my everyday environment more pleasant (e.g., put a support on my chair, placed a meaningful photo on my desk)	1	2	3	4	5
I did things to make my work setting more enjoyable (e.g., planned fun Fridays, partnered with a co-worker on an assignment)	1	2	3	4	5

Total _____

Average for Subscale = Total/# of items _____

Self-Compassion (SC) – 7 items

I noticed, *without judgment*, when I was struggling (e.g., feeling resistance, falling short of my goals, not completing as much as I'd like)	1	2	3	4	5
I punitively/harshly judged my progress and effort *reverse scored*	5	4	3	2	1
I kindly acknowledged my own challenges and difficulties	1	2	3	4	5
I engaged in critical or harsh self-talk *reverse scored*	5	4	3	2	1
I engaged in supportive and comforting self-talk (e.g., "My effort is valuable and meaningful")	1	2	3	4	5
I reminded myself that failure and challenge are part of the human experience	1	2	3	4	5

I gave myself permission to feel my feelings (e.g., allowed myself to cry)   1   2   3   4   5

Total _____

Average for Subscale = Total/# of items _____

Spiritual Practice (SP) – 6 items

I experienced meaning and/or a larger purpose in my _work/school_ life (e.g., for a cause)   1   2   3   4   5

I experienced meaning and/or a larger purpose in my _private/personal_ life (e.g., for a cause)   1   2   3   4   5

I spent time in a spiritual place (e.g., church, meditation room, nature)   1   2   3   4   5

I read, watched, or listened to something inspirational (e.g., watched a video that gives me hope, read inspirational material, listened to spiritual music)   1   2   3   4   5

I spent time with others who share my spiritual worldview (e.g., church community, volunteer group)   1   2   3   4   5

I spent time doing something that I hope will make a positive difference in the world (e.g., volunteered at a soup kitchen, took time out for someone else)   1   2   3   4   5

Total _____

Average for Subscale = Total/# of items _____

General (G) – 3 items

I engaged in a variety of self-care strategies (e.g., mindfulness, support, exercise, nutrition, spiritual practice)   1   2   3   4   5

I planned my self-care   1   2   3   4   5

I explored new ways to bring self-care into my life   1   2   3   4   5

Total _____

Average for Subscale = Total/# of items _____

Total Score Summary
Be sure you have correctly scored your *reverse scored* items

Averaged Score	Subscale
_____	Nutrition/Hydration (NH)
_____	Exercise (E)
_____	Self-Soothing (S)
_____	Self-Awareness/Mindfulness (SA)
_____	Rest (R)
_____	Relationships (RR)
_____	Physical/Medical (PM)
_____	Environmental Factors (EF)
_____	Self-Compassion (SC)
_____	Spiritual Practice (SP)
_____	General (G)

Shade in your average score for each subscale below:

```
5
4
3
2
1
Scale   NH   E   S   SA   R   RR   PM   SC   SP   G
```

3

The Impact of Teacher Self-Care on Students

"Teachers influence their students not only by how and what they teach but also by how they relate, teach and model social and emotional constructs, and manage the classroom" (Jennings & Greenberg, 2009, p. 499). Intuitively, administrators and educators know that self-care is good for teachers' efficacy and for their personal quality of life. Unfortunately, for some, this may not be motivation enough to take steps towards self-care. We also know that self-care strengthens personal and family relationships. The benefits of self-care for teachers in their professional lives, however, may still go unnoticed or be underappreciated. We might find the motivation to take care of ourselves and declare it as a top priority if we see all of the other added advantages, namely the improvement in student learning and school climates.

Many teachers can relate to the days when we start the day or week already rundown, and things seem to spiral downwards in the classroom as well. Your lousy night's sleep, the traffic accident on the way to school, or a sick family member can mean our students will feel your stress, too. Hattie and

Yates' (2014) *Visible Learning and the Science of How We Learn* supports this notion:

> Many studies have been published into what is called the chameleon effect. This refers to the fact that when people are in close proximity, a level of mimicry occurs; even though none of the parties may be aware this is taking place. Significantly, the quality of the relationship relates to the level of mimicry. People who cooperate and get on well have shown a high level of this behavioral mirroring. Studies also found that this type of mimicry still will take place even when there is little genuine basis for the relationship, with the other person merely being in the same room at the time. In fact, mimicry is so automatic that it normally increases when people are placed under conditions of cognitive load.
>
> (p. 274)

So by a teacher's daily presence alone, even before introducing direct instruction in wellness strategies, students are absorbing and mimicking the habits of coping or reacting to everyday stresses. Whether a teacher makes a conscious effort or not to put their well-being as a priority, the teacher's default emotional and mental state will affect the students and the climate they are inhabiting and creating together.

A teacher's chronic state of stress might seem like an issue a teacher can compartmentalize for outside the classroom or shield in some way from their students and colleagues. This might even be applauded as a spectacular feat of strength and courage to muscle through our days serving our students first even if we are feeling burnout. You might have a visual of popular teacher memes that circulate of a split photo of a fresh, well-groomed teacher in August on one side and a haggardly disheveled teacher by May on the other side. What's harder to see in a meme is that day-to-day effect of teacher's interactions and rapport with students. Hattie and Yates (2014) warn that,

> the evidence suggests that, within any teaching situation, your interpersonal gestures and bodily movements assumed enormous importance in the brains of your students (i.e., physiologically). What has been established through the laboratory studies is that the use of physical gesture, hand movement, and facial expression all contribute strongly to the mental activity people will experience as they watch another person behave.
>
> (p. 277)

This makes the well-being of teachers and its outward signs (body language, gestures, tone, expression) of the utmost importance in the lives of our students.

Sometimes it is hard to track or see these effects because there are several stages between a teacher's intentional care for themselves and a student's success or progress. A teacher's self-care practice, for example, might set them up to have the patience and the capacity to connect with students more frequently. As Jennings and Greenberg (2009) emphasize: "Supportive relationships with teachers can promote feelings of safety and connectedness among students, providing the social support necessary to thrive socially, emotionally, and academically" (p. 501). Often, we know a teacher will not see the effects of their teaching on their students themselves and hope and wonder what became of so many students. Hattie and Yates point out that "a recent American study found that marked improvements in student achievement occurred not in the year the program was carried out, but in the year following the intervention, with student grades improving nine percentile points in the targeted students" (p. 17). The delayed benefits make teacher self-care and, consequently, teacher–student relationships challenging to recognize at that moment without extensive and long-term tracking of students. It is no wonder that self-care is not sticking as a priority (for teachers, but for school culture as well) as its benefits on students and schools often remain invisible to us.

Despite this difficulty in making the teacher–student wellness connection visible, we are increasingly seeing that teacher self-care does, indeed, lead to changes in their students, classrooms, and school. Seeing real cases of how the well-being of teachers has improved students' lives and school communities may finally be the catalyst for teachers (and our educational systems) to begin taking care of teachers more seriously. Here are inspiring instances where teachers who took care of themselves saw their schools and students benefit as well.

A second-grade teacher practices closing her eyes and breathing deeply when she is feeling stressed in her classroom. She has shared that she tells the students she is taking a moment for herself. It helps her to stay calm so that she is present for her students. At that moment, she is not worrying if her students are also practicing. She is taking a moment for herself.

A middle-school teacher has students write in their journals about how they're feeling after recess. She spends the time writing in her journal, noticing where she's at emotionally at this point in the day. The energy in the classroom has shifted dramatically since she began implementing the journal and she has found that she has more energy and positive interactions for the remainder of the day.

A high-school teacher often takes deep breaths when she encounters stressful situations in the classroom. Practicing deep breaths doesn't necessarily make her feel less frustrated, but doing so allows her to stay calm and in control.

Teachers report that they have heard students tell them that they see their teacher "taking a break" with a quick head massage or a deep breath. They've shared that sometimes teachers need a break, too and have become more sensitive to their teachers' feelings.

In a middle-school classroom, some students were exhibiting less than desirable behavior choices. Before approaching the students, the teacher practiced a few deep breaths to make sure she stayed regulated. While she was doing this, she overheard a female student say to another "Why isn't she yelling at them to stop?" The other student replied, "This is the teacher who doesn't yell. She does that breathing thing instead." Hearing the side conversations of the two young ladies hit home that students are observing how we as teachers are handling ourselves in stressful situations.

Many teachers conflate behavior management, social-emotional learning, mindfulness, and self-care practices. Thinking that if they "lose their cool" in front of students or "own" their stress and anxiety that they have failed. On the contrary, it is those educators who can articulte their emotions and model appropriate self-care and coping strategies who are not only creating safe, constructive classrooms for learning, but are also effectivley managing these classrooms by modeling positive ways to handle negative emotions giving their students the life skills they need to succeed in both the home and school environments.

Modeling self-care and building relaxation into the school day can be simple and easy. There is no need to rearrange desks or burn through instructional minutes with lengthy transitions. Included below are two simple relaxation activities, by Elias Patras, that can help dysregulated students, adults, and stakeholders who need a moment to pause and get centered.

Activity: Be the Tree

Close your eyes and take a breath in. Slowly allow yourself to relax as you exhale. You can sense that you start to relax from your toes up.

Wiggle your toes and breath, allow each breath, each wiggle to let go of any stress in your toes and feet. With each breath in and out allow yourself to slowly relax even deeper. Take another breath in and out. Allow your legs to relax, your hips, your torso and arms. Move your neck slowly, release all tension in your neck and head. Take a deeper breath in and out. As you feel your body relaxing, visualize yourself emersed in nature. When you look around, you see an amazing large tree. Notice its beauty, its strong trunk, branches, and how tall and large this tree is. Notice its branches and how they expand wide into the sky above you. As you get closer to this tree, see yourself merging with the tree, you and the tree become one. Your legs become the roots of the tree, your body becomes the trunk, your arms become the branches. You can feel your roots go deep into the ground. Down through the dirt all the way down to the center of the Earth. See your roots being strong, solid and well grounded. Imagine, if you will, your body, the trunk of the tree, how strong this center is, how solid. Now notice your branches how they expand, how they are able to hold many leaves, and wild life. See how these branches expand even higher up, all the way into the sky, into the clouds. See how you are part of nature, earth, and the sky above. Focus on your breath and when you are feeling larger than you can imagine with your tree, take that all in, and breathe again.

Activity: Climb the Mountain

Take a calming breath in and slowly exhale out. Take another breath and slowly exhale out. If is accessible and feels safe, close your eyes. See yourself on a beautiful mountain, surrounded by the green of the land. There is a path on this mountain, and you decide to take it. The walk is easy and effortless, with each step you have a sense of purpose, a sense of accomplishment. Not knowing what will be at the top of the mountain but knowing you will have achieved going to the top of this mountain with ease. You are about a quarter of the way up, and as you look down you can see the forest the trees and realize that with each breath in and out, this journey was easy. You continue to go up the mountain and you see birds flying and soaring effortlessly. You notice that you are halfway up this mountain. The path is clear. The climb is easy. You are not out of breath but feel energized. As you continue your climb you can see footprints on the path. Others have traveled here before. Your footprint doesn't fit these footprints but they are similar in shape. It is comforting to know that this climb has been done by others before you. You notice even more footprints but they stop somewhere closer to the top. As you look down you can hardly see the trees. They look like pretty sticks standing straight up. You no longer see the footprints but you do see the top of the mountain. You have arrived. The top of the mountain is very green. The air is cool but refreshing. And at this moment you realized that you made this climb, it was effortless. Take a breath in and slowly exhale. Stretch your arms upward and as you lower them, open your eyes if they were closed.

Support from Stress: What the Research Says

Kiljoong Kim, PhD
Senior Policy Analyst, University of Chicago

Despite a series of research suggesting serious intervention for teacher stress as early as 1980s and onward (Cox, Boot, Cox, & Harrison, 1988; Guglielmi & Tatrow, 1998; Hall, Woodhouse, & Wooster, 1986; Kovess-Masféty, Rios-Seidel, & Sevilla-Dedieu, 2007), according to the participants of Mindful Practices professional development sessions, it is quite evident that there is a glaring absence of institutional support from schools and districts when it comes to managing stress for school-level staff. This includes teachers, counselors, and administrators (Table 3.1). Previous research defines teacher stress as depression, burnout, physical illness and poor quality of life leading to decreased retention (Fantuzzo et al., 2012; Yang, Ge, Hu, Chi, & Wang, 2009). Highly individualized remedies for stress (e.g., reading, exercising, drinking) means that many teachers are momentarily walking away from a potentially toxic work environment to deal with their stress only to find themselves returning to the same condition and repeat the venomous cycle. Furthermore, a recent study indicated that even institutionalized support such as professional development as the implementation of evidence-based classroom interventions could have minimal to no impact on reducing teacher stress (Ouellette et al., 2018). While there is tremendous irony given that teachers have long been providers of mental health services for students (Green et al., 2013; Rones & Hoagwood, 2000), such predicaments with unresolved working conditions lead many school administrators to deal with their stressed staff through such simplistic resolutions as giving them more time off away from schools or by seeking help without proper evaluation of their impact.

TABLE 3.1 Qualitative Responses to Reduce their Own Stress

Category	Sub-categories	Description	Examples	Notes on coding
Exercise/ Sports/ Active recreation		Physical activity	Exercise, work out, yoga	Yoga is double coded as exercise and meditation
Meditation/ Mindfulness	Formal meditation	Mentions of meditation or a meditation practice	Meditate, yoga	Yoga is double coded as exercise and meditation
	Relaxation techniques	Relaxation or meditation not in a formal framework	Deep breathing, relaxation	
	Reflection		Thinking about the day, journaling	
	Creative	A hobby or outlet that involves creativity or arts	Painting, writing	Dance is double coded as creative and exercise
Recreational activity (non-exercise/ sports)	Social	A hobby or outlet that involves being with others	Volunteering, participating in club activities	
	Home/ House	A hobby or outlet that takes place in the home or is directed at the home	Cooking, cleaning	
Time with family and friends	Spouse Family Friends	Any mention of family or friends		Activities such as "take a walk with a friend" are coded as Active recreation/Time with friends
Time alone		Mentions of being alone	Spend time alone, take a relaxing bath	
Eating/ Drinking			Beer, drink wine	Flag for alcohol consumption

(Kim, 2018)

As is the case with many efforts in education, teachers' self-care is an iterative process without a silver bullet. That is, the painstaking efforts to raise awareness, determining what works, streamlining and institutionalizing so that self-care becomes a part of school/district culture require a great deal of planning and continuous evaluation at every step. Applying the lenses of Continuous Quality Improvement (CQI), an ongoing process that evaluates what works and does not work to improve its processes, can create a culture of reflection and learning that can adapt along with the school whenever its staff or culture shifts. In fact, the same research that found evidence-based classroom interventions ineffective found organizational health including teacher connectedness to be the significant predictor for teacher stress and satisfaction (Ouellette et al., 2018). While school climate is heavily emphasized when it comes to the academic performance of students and their well-being, and the same degree of emphasis on climate exists for creating or sustaining a school, teacher-centered measures of school climate do not exist when it comes to the performance of teachers.

In order for leaders to consider a more structured, direct approach to deal with teachers' stress, evaluation of initiatives, programs, or interventions can provide valuable information. This structured approach is particularly important given significant differences in teacher stress by various sociodemographic characteristics such as age, experience/rank, gender, and geography, and various other school conditions including resources, density, student behavior, and accountability policies (Atkins, Graczyk, Frazier, & Adil, 2003; Borg, Riding, & Falzon, 1991; Brown & Ralph, 1992; Cappella, Frazier, Atkins, Schoenwald, & Glisson, 2008; Laughlin, 1984; Pierce & Molloy, 1990; Punch & Tuettemann, 1990; Shernoff, Mehta, Atkins, Torf, & Spencer, 2011).

Education is a unique field and industry in that there is a persistent underlying belief that all activities ought to ultimately lead to positive student outcomes. While such belief may be considered noble, it also places daunting pressure on those who are accountable for student academics. Despite such a pressured environment, unlike many other professions, research shows evidence that financial incentives do not necessarily retain teachers and their emotional attachment to students play a significant role in their motives and longevity (Lam, 2019). But given that enhancing their work environment plays a key role, the next step is for policymakers and leaders in the field to facilitate the mechanism to achieve a good environment including holding administrators accountable not only for academic performance but for creating a climate in which both students and teachers feel connected.

4

Implementation and Support for Well-Being

As we read in Chapter 1, teachers are under tremendous stress, and our educational systems are not providing well-being supports like other industries. As a nation, our data on student and teacher well-being is daunting. Increased suicide rates and fear of gun violence for both students and teachers has left districts scrabbling for solutions. When the issues facing districts are so weighty, it can feel impossible to categorize them with any importance. Is it that our sense of urgency is missing? Have we become complacent? Or rather, we would argue that this is an issue of decreased capacity instead of complacency.

We see many school districts either experiencing initiative paralysis or initiative overdrive. The fear is that beginning with one thing, such as well-being, might appear to some like we are ignoring other significant issues that should take precedence. Conversely, the "shotgun" approach leaves us with multiple layers of task forces, committees, PLCs, BHTs, ILTs – and other assorted acronyms – all with similar goals, timelines, and myriad Google Docs. While these are all important, if not done well the result leaves us all too tired to be creative or to take on "one more thing," even our self-care.

To begin, we must decide to prioritize teacher well-being and move forward without apology. We must end a culture of complicity within our school cultures. We are not prioritizing teacher well-being at the expense of other pressing student issues. We are taking care of the people that take care of students. There will be more success with all other initiatives and goals if our teachers are at their best. We care best for our youth when we care about the teachers that serve our youth.

We know that teachers who practice and implement self-care need encouragement and support to sustain their efforts even when they and others see the benefits of implementing mindfulness in their personal and professional life. In Chapter 3 we saw that when teachers grow in their understanding and practice of self-care, the impact on their classroom experience and their students becomes more and more apparent to other teachers, administrators, students, and students' families. Now how do we bring these individual success stories into a systemic movement of positive change?

The good news is that these positive individuals are naturally inspiring others around them. Over and over again in our work with teachers and schools across the country, we see this happen. When colleagues see their peers handling stress more effectively, more relaxed, and enjoying their students more, even a little bit more, they want to know how this is happening and how they can have the same experiences.

To build on this naturally contagious phenomenon, we can forge even stronger teacher alliances and supports with more intention. Let's not rest on isolated, sporadic victories. Let's build a grassroots support system to make intentional changes to the system at the school, district, state, and national level. Let's make this a concerted and organized push. Our focus now is on opportunities for systemic teacher support in school systems.

Informal Opportunities for Intentionality Building Community

In the beginning, this may still look like isolated individuals making changes for just their daily well-being and mood. These informal opportunities might look like:

◆ Cultivating the pause or any short moments that bring you back – (it could be every time you sit at your desk, or walk to the copy room, or set dedicated moments at scheduled points throughout your day)
◆ Breathwork while cutting vegetables
◆ Taking a breath before opening the door
◆ Walking to work or taking a walk during a break
◆ Reaching out to a colleague once a day with a positive comment
◆ Taking five minutes of meditation at lunch instead of checking your phone
◆ Noticing more closely during any sensory moments (wiping the whiteboard clean, pushing in chairs, sorting folders)
◆ Setting an intention or dedicating a day or class period to a student
◆ Taking short hallway walks during your plan periods
◆ Devoting self-care time before or after the school day
◆ Inviting a colleague to join you

Remember that one person's informal practice is not someone else's. Also, if you are going to be doing something anyway, add the intentionality, without adding the time to your day. This way it becomes a form of practice and not just another thing to pile on your to-do list.

Included below are two breath work activities that teachers, practioners, and school stakeholders can use daily. These visualization activities, developed by Elias Patras, are rooted in nature and help educators be present in the moment by focusing on the very core of their being, their breath.

Activity: Breathe in the Breeze

Take a deep breath. Pause. Slowly exhale out. Be intentional about your breathing. Slowly close your eyes, if closing your eyes feels accessible and safe. If not, focus your gaze on a spot on the floor. Take another deep breath in and slowly exhale out. Follow this with another breath in and slowly exhale out. Now imagine that you are in your favorite place in nature, it's relaxing and calming. You can see that it's a beautiful sunny day. You can almost sense a warm breeze surrounding you. This breeze starts at your feet. As your feel the breeze at your feet, you can feel your feet relax, as the breeze whisks away the tension that you keep here. You can sense, or feel, this beautiful breeze as it hits your legs, taking away the stress of the day that you might have. You can now feel it on your hips, removing all tension here. This breeze travels up your body to your stomach and whole torso and arms, allowing you to feel relaxed and calm. Traveling up to your neck and head, having this amazing breeze blow out any tension that is stored in your head or neck. Now you can sense or feel the breeze blow around you, releasing any left-over tension or anxiety that you might have. With a final breath in, slowly exhale out and release all that is left of that uneasiness. Slowly come back to the here and now and breathe naturally.

Activity: Breathe in the Sun

Take a deep breath. Pause. Slowly exhale out. Be intentional about your breathing. Slowly close your eyes, if closing your eyes feels accessible and safe. If not, focus your gaze on a spot on the floor.

Take another deep breath in and slowly exhale out. Follow this with another breath in and slowly exhale out. Now imagine that you are in a place of nature, it's relaxing and calming. You can see that it's a beautiful sunny day. Focus on the sun, this beautiful ball of orange glow. Feel the sun's rays coming down hitting the top of your head, giving you a sense of peace and calm. Moving down to your forehead, releasing any tension, overthinking, or stress in this area. As these beautiful sunshine rays of gold come through, you can feel the warmth on your throat allowing yourself to communicate clearly, coming on down and shining upon the center of your chest, warming your heart and expanding your places of the heart that you share with others and yourself. The sun shines a bit more brightly as you feel it on your stomach and as it goes down to your toes. Feeling a warmth or a glow of peace and relaxation. Take another deep breath in as you look in your mind, picturing the sun and sharing a smile in gratitude for the wonders of nature that the sun brings. Open your eyes and smile. Feel the glow that you created inside of yourself on the outside.

Because teachers often feel very isolated, it is essential to make the most of the quick opportunities to connect with colleagues. This could include the short chats walking from the parking lot to the building, in line to use the copy machine, waiting for students to file out of assemblies, or grabbing a bite in the lounge. Just taking a moment to share your intention to be mindful with a colleague sets a powerful tone in the school community. This is one of many intentional moments that can start a ripple of change.

When teachers get a break and choose to visit one another, this is another opportunity to go negative or positive. One teacher we worked with committed to giving a compliment each day to someone in the building. If she overheard students talking about a positive experience they had in a colleague's classroom, she would make a point to pass it on to the teacher. With energy and time at a premium in a teacher's day, small efforts can make an enormous difference, especially when there are few opportunities.

We worked with one school district where the superintendent asked all employees, including her, not just teachers, to be paired with a buddy. Throughout the school year, they would check in with their buddy at least once per week. By the end of the school year, people connected in ways that they never imagined.

One recommended strategy for checking in with a buddy is a three-part process: celebration, inspiration, action. Celebrate something positive you experienced, either something in your classroom or something you observed in the school. Share an inspiration, a small step you are inspired to take. Not something you feel you "should" do but something that will bring you lightness or joy; something as small as giving yourself and another person a sticker, or the compliment-a-day plan. For example, one administrator we worked with, once a month would go around with a sheet of silly stickers, pop in to say hi, hand out a sticker, and that was it. No evaluation, no assignment, nothing more than a sticker visit. This brought him and staff joy every time, it was his small step. Once you decide what your small step with be, let your buddy know what you are inspired to do and what support you might need to make it happen. Buddies close the check-in by saying to one another: "I will support you by _____. And I look forward to celebrating with you next time." Take action to do it so that you have your celebration ready the next time you see your buddy.

Whole School Implementation and Support

In many districts, administrator compassion fatigue is on par with the teacher burnout and, sadly, it is often administrators who unknowingly perpetuate a system of dysfunction in their school communities. Long hours and isolation often define the role of a school administrator; these conditions often lead to an empathetic failure on their part to see, without bias, the needs of their faculty and staff. Put differently: if burnt out teachers are depersonalizing their students, exhausted administrators are depersonalizing their teachers. They become unknowingly complicit in the system of dysfunction.

When looking to implement well-being practices across a school district, the mission is to start with intentionality. Define well-being at the individual system level, for every stakeholder in the building. What does practicing, modelling, and messaging well-being "look like" for the district leaders, teachers, para-professionals, security guards, school clerks, parents, and students? What does it mean to practice well-being for yourself and model and message it for others? Taking a page from our work with Social-Emotional Learning, these questions are rooted in each stakeholder cultivating self-awareness, first by learning from self-assessment and the practice of regulating behavior daily.

There are a number of tools easily embedded in the school day without adding more to anyone's workload. The steps below are a great start:

◆ School-wide Well-being Calendar.
◆ Breathwork at meeting start.
◆ Voluntary Teacher Buddies.
◆ Mobilize around the goal, teacher well-being, with a sense of urgency. Name a Call to Action. Design a one-pager: info-graphic, call to action, core beliefs, mission, vision, timeline, and goals.
◆ Build a task force of stakeholders with clear directives. Decide upfront how progress will be measured and collect that data (i.e., teacher attrition rates will go down, teacher satisfaction rates will go up).
◆ Provide a menu of well-being practices, both individual and social, both relaxing and invigorating (i.e., yoga, mindfulness, game of basketball, coffee with friends, etc.). There is no right or wrong way to access well-being practices; the critical piece is that they become a practice.

- ◆ Connect students and teachers (tools like Class Catalyst).
- ◆ Reflect and begin again with a single growth point. A single call to action that everyone can articulate and everyone will be able to see objectively when the goal is reached.

Not only will these strategies not be adding to the workload of anyone, they also will not feel mandatory or like another chore weighing teachers down. The schools will most likely find buy-in when they focus on providing the optimal space for teachers to find that practice. Instead of another item on the agenda, it is a sweet, enticing resource to fold into your day, whenever the teacher is ready or motivated. Schools should focus on and be the space holder and the library. You can't make them check out the book, but you can make them feel excited about checking out the book.

Reflection Questions for School-Wide Support of Educator Self-Care

These questions are intended to generate open sharing and non-judgmental listening of individuals' experience and perspective on the issues and impact of educator self-care, to move your learning community toward a collaborative approach to increasing the well-being of all educators.

1. What have you learned about the needs of educators from reading *Everyday Self-Care for Educators: Tools and Strategies for Well-Being*?
2. In what ways does your experience resonate with some of the emotional and physical impacts of teaching and working with children described in the research cited?
3. What moments during the day or week or school year do you notice that teacher self-care is needed most?
4. What challenging areas of teachers' lives in and out of the school day are opportunities for change and self-care?
5. Imagine what your school community might look and feel like if it cultivates a culture of self-care and wellness. Describe or imagine the details.
6. Who are the colleagues you think of first in your school community that you can take the first steps in sharing this message of self-care or buddying up with to support each other?
7. Who are the people or communities outside your school building or community that can be non-judgmental and neutral support to your professional and personal wellness?
8. What are some concrete actions or changes your school can take to create a culture of mindfulness and self-care?

9. How often are staff affirmations a regular and formal part of the school day?
10. Are opportunities for short mindfulness breaks actively encouraged by administration?
11. Are brief self-care strategies regularly a topic that has five minutes of the agenda in professional development (PD)/professional learning community (PLC) opportunities?
12. Is there a formal wellness champion or social events coordinator (or a similar position) on staff?

When colleagues or teams gather for discussion, using some or all of the following agreements can help establish a safe environment, conducive to open sharing and non-judgmental listening.

Agreements

1. Be fully present – suspend phones and eliminate distractions
2. Be willing to experience discomfort – tolerate lack of closure
3. Keep an open mind
4. Listen actively
5. Assume good intent
6. Share your truth
7. Watch your air time

Conclusion

As we put the finishing touches on this book, another large school district has announced a teachers' strike this week. If the canaries fleeing the coal mines are our gauge, then it appears our system is in crisis. We live in a country that values education, but does not value the well-being of our educators.

Sadly, the conversation around this educational crisis has become all too familiar, predictable, and mundane. It has become the background to our educational tableau. We all sit motionless and frozen in the conventional wisdom of the age, while the needs at the center of our crisis, those of our teachers, do not hold our attention longer than it takes Channel 7 to pack up their news camera and head home.

This conventional wisdom dictates the conversation around teacher needs lands somewhere between summers off, merit pay, and class sizes. While all these issues are important, this conversation has become stale, and often misses the concept of well-being altogether.

Education has become accustomed to the framed, quick fixes of "7 Habits of X" or "5 Steps to Y" or "3 Solutions for Z" all of which are theoretically workable within that safe, conventional wisdom of our current system. We want change so we listen to the talks, we buy the books, and we laminate the posters all without challenging the current thinking which is, in this case, that students' achievement must frame the conversation leaving everything else, including those things that are critical to that achievement, as afterthoughts.

It is almost as if we a fear a departure from this conventional wisdom would open up a Pandora's box of teacher resentments that we, as a system, would not be able to shut. If we host the occasional teacher wellness day with a salad bar and an inspirational speaker we can engage in the willing suspension of disbelief that this talisman will safeguard against the burnout, isolation, depersonalization, compassion fatigue, and emotional exhaustion that is causing teachers and administrators (as administration attrition rates are also alarmingly high) to leave the profession in droves.

Of course, this talisman doesn't work. We are taking an aspirin for a stomach ache. The result is that education is experiencing its own type of Brexit. Neither teachers nor administrators are 100% certain of the factors that have gotten them here or the path that lays in front of them, they just want to take back control and extrication feels like the only way.

Kids don't say that they want to be teachers anymore, because teaching just doesn't look fun. College students don't declare education as a major anymore, because the vague promise of impacting lives doesn't convincingly counterbalance the realities of the twenty-first-century classroom or the weight of student loans. Those holding up our schools have been departing at a rate that we have become so cozy with we forgot that it would be cause for alarm in almost any other industry besides nursing.

Teachers have been leaving education for years, but with plenty of teachers there was no need for us to pay attention. We were able to hire all the teachers we needed. We turned a blind eye to teacher needs and kept the conversation centered around student needs. We are not listening to John Hattie and investing resources in those who have caring relationships with our students.

How did we find ourselves here? Instead of looking to the root cause, some of us are doubling down on spending district resources on teacher recruitment. Spending dollars to recruit new educators instead of retaining the high-quality, dedicated teachers and staff that we already have. Instead of changing our structures to honor the needs of the people that are already in our buildings who, most importantly, have already formed the invaluable connections with our students that make them want to come to school, stay in school and learn, we spend money recruiting new faces.

A critical first step lies in the power of naming the problem. Shifting the narrative from discussing only students' needs to also prioritizing the well-being needs of our teachers in a consistent and meaningful way. Not because teacher and administrator suicide rates are cause for alarm, which they are. Not because teacher and administrator retention rates are cause for alarm, which they are. But because it is our obligation to care about the well-being of those that have given their lives to our country's youth. Not a legal obligation, but a moral one.

Call to Action: We Must Take Care of Those that Take Care of Our Students

Continue the conversation with Carla by visiting ITeachBecause. com! ITeachBecause.com is a free platform, to connect teachers and school stakeholders to inspire and get inspired.

Carla and her team created ITeachBecause.com to break down the isolation between teachers and their colleagues and give voice to their victories and challenges. By joining the free, online community participants open the door to inspiring others and being inspired. Sharing our stories helps us all remember not only why we teach but also that we are part of a larger community.

Teaching can be a lonely profession. Often when we close the door, it is just us and the students. People don't have to feel alone. Let's move past our silos and champion the message of school stakeholders across the country and help advocate for teachers in Washington.

We all have horrible and wonderful stories. Tales that don't only belong to a high-school teacher in Iowa or a PE teacher in Brooklyn, but to all of us.

Our challenges – just like our successes – are shared and need to become part of our national conversation on education, if we are going to have real conversations about the well-being of our educators. Moving from tired conventional wisdom and remarks of "those that can't do," to honoring the needs and well-being of those that CAN do.

Idealistic? Yes. But, without idealism there would be no social progress.

Let the take away from this book be more than practicing tree pose or a mindful breath each day. Instead, let it be something just as fun, but more noble.

Mobilize as a community of caring adults who work in schools. Advocate for educator well-being. Create a collective community. Shift the climate and culture of education. Move past the conventional wisdom of teachers vs. students.

If you don't have time to start your own community, then join our ITeachBecause.com community and lift up one another. It is more than a collection of individual stories. It is a collection of voices, a chorus of inspiration and shared challenges woven together to illuminate the needs of today's teacher. Share your story and inspire thousands of educators, administrators, and school stakeholders across the country. It doesn't matter what your background is, your race, your gender, what town you are from, what your politics are, if you are a PC or Mac person, if you have purple hair, or a unicorn horn we are all educators who need our voices to be heard and our well-being needs met.

If it were 1968 we would take to the streets. But in 2019 we mobilize in a different way – our tweets, our shares – to spread the word, raise awareness to tell our story so it doesn't get drowned out or muddled in politics or agendas. Now, we need to learn the lessons of other movements, like Occupy – it fizzled, because no one knew what they were working toward. What are we working toward?

What's our goal? One million voices who have joined the ITeachBecause.com community. One million people who have shared stories across the country. One million teachers and school stakeholders coming together to reinvigorate their passion for teaching. And we will keep going until one million voices have been heard!

We MUST harness the power of the community narrative.

In today's political age, we need to change the way lawmakers view education and the well-being needs of our educators. We have to remove the barriers and get school stakeholders, policy makers, legislators, and teachers on the same page. We have a moral imperative to give our students and our teachers the well-being tools they need to succeed – not just in school, but in life. We need to deliver on solutions for the caring adults in our school buildings who get out of bed every morning to do this tough and important work.

Idealistic? Yes. But, without idealism there would be no social progress.

Connection and conversation is how we sustain ourselves as a movement and shift the national dialogue. Can we change the education industry? Can we put teacher well-being at the center of the education conversation? Yes. Think seat belts.

Sixty years ago people didn't care about seat belts, never mind car seats. Conventional wisdom was that people wouldn't wear seat belts. No interest. In fact, legislators had to fight to convince us all otherwise. Now, we would never even think about getting in without buckling up and making sure our adults and children were secured. The very thought is ludicrous.

As an industry, education, let's be on the right side of history here. Let's get a place where taking care of those who take care of our students is the new standard. We see the problems in education. We need to own the solutions. This is our seat belt moment: Education. Let's seize it!

By stating that we acknowledge the well-being needs of our teachers and students collectively, we create the space to move past the convenient conventional wisdom of the day. Let education be the paragon of equity in these polarizing political times. Let all voices that create a school's climate and culture be heard. Let's move the past teachers vs. students vs. administrators vs. support staff mentality that has dominated educational culture for years. No longer one need over the other; both needs are highlighted. By addressing the needs of the teachers we uplift the students as well.

Another step in addressing the needs of teachers and school stakeholders is providing time for educators to share openly about their successes and struggles. In this tough, crazy, draining climate in education, many teachers, school stakeholders, and administrators find themselves asking why they teach. Let's face it, the job is tough.

In her work across the country, Carla went on a listening tour asking these very questions:

Why do you teach?
Is your well-being a priority to your school?
Do you connect with your colleagues daily?

Carla noticed that engaging school partners in conversations about why they do what they do, what challenges they endure and what successes they can celebrate created a bridge that brought them together. By not limiting "teaching" to the delivery of academic content – but to anyone in a school building who teaches a student how to be their best self in the world – she allowed every caring adult in the school building to be part of the conversation.

These conversations were transformative for school partners, moving them beyond conventional wisdom and quick fixes to balanced solutions that address both students' and teachers' well-being needs equally. It didn't matter what role the adult played, the type of school, or where it was located. Teachers all teach because they want the best life for their students, they all face challenges in reaching that goal and those challenges often negatively impact their well-being.

We have found that those districts that have the most success including teacher self-care into the fabric of their climate culture do two things well: they plan together and they practice together. First, when planning together, they come up with 3-, 6-, 12-, and 18-month tangible, intentional goals. These goals do not live in "Google docs," these goals are known by all stakeholders across the school community. Second, these succesful districts practice well-being strategies in ever corner of every school building. This does not mean they all get out yoga mats every day (although that would be great!), instead they do simply things: starting every faculty meeting with a 3-minute centering activity, ending every team meeting with a one-word check out. What makes these districts successful is they see this planning and practice infused in the climate and culture of their school buildings. Teachers feel more comfortable including well-being practices into their daily routines because their principal is leading them through those same practices during weekly faculty meetings. Self-care moves from smelling of compliance to feeling, and being, a priority for all.

Included below are some sample well-being activities adapted from Carla's Social-Emotional Learning series *Everyday SEL* (Routledge). These strategies can be practiced, along with the activities in previous chapters, to begin or end a faculty meeting, by individual teachers who would like to take a moment to pause or by any adult or child who is in need of a moment to center.

Activity: Memory Minute

Facilitator will turn off all screens, projectors, computers in the room and will cue participants to turn off and put away all personal devices. The facilitator will instruct all stakeholders to visualize a blank sheet of paper and clear their minds of all thoughts. The facilitator will cue stakeholders to place one hand on their stomachs and one hand on their collarbones to follow the rhythm of their breath (without the need to control it). Setting the timer for one minute, the faciliator will give stakeholders the option of closing their eyes as they sit together in stillness and breathe.

Activity: Owning My Story Journal

Stakeholders each receive a piece of scrap paper or index card. The facilitator sets a timer for two minutes. The stakeholders each draw their response to the prompt, "Today, my self-care story is ..." Each stakeholder will write their well-being successes and challenges from a place of observation not judgment. When the two minutes has concluded, each stakeholder will pause to read what they wrote. On the back of their paper or index card, they will write a simple goal that they can accomplish in the next two weeks to help meet their sample self-care needs, such as going to yoga class, or taking at least 30 minutes to connect with a co-worker.

Activity: One-Word Check-in/Check-out

Stakeholders form a circle. Select a stakeholder to open the activity. They will share one word that reflects something they are grateful for/inspired by/feeling in that moment. Moving to the left, each person will share a word until each person in the circle has shared. (People may opt to skip their turn, merely by saying "Pass.")

Activity: Drawing Out Loud

Stakeholders each receive a piece of scrap paper or index card. The facilitator sets a timer for two minutes. The stakeholders each draw their response to a prompt relevant to the theme of the meeting/current events. Sample themes could be "Compassion toward self and others," "Boundaries for myself with others," "Balance between my needs and the needs of my students," or "Self-care for me and my students." When the two minutes is up, each stakeholder turns to the person next to them to share their drawings. (People may opt to skip their turn, merely by saying "Pass.")

It is our intention that the tools in this book will hopefully create a bridge to bring your school community together, rallying around the importance of teacher and student well-being. By providing our readers with not only the "why" behind the work, but also practical, easy-to-implement strategies that illuminate the path to "how" as well. Well-being starts with teachers and school stakeholders, who own the work and model practices, successes, and learning from failures daily. Educator well-being is not about perfection – it is about being true to who we are and what we need so that our students can find the courage to do the same.

References

Arens, A. K. & Morin, A. J. S. (2016). Relations between teachers' emotional exhaustion and students' educational outcomes. *Journal of Educational Psychology*, 108(6), 800–813.

Atkins, M., Graczyk, P., Frazier, S., & Adil, J. (2003). Toward a new model for school-based mental health: Accessible, effective, and sustainable services in urban communities. *School Psychology Review*, 32, 503–514.

Barrett, M. (2011, December 12). *Lecture Presented at Center for Contextual Change*. Skokie, IL.

Bellingrath, S., Weigl, T., & Kudielka, B. M. (2009). Chronic work stress and exhaustion is associated with higher allostatic load in female teachers. *Stress: The International Journal on the Biology of Stress*, 12(1), 37–48.

Bernard, M. E. (2016). Teacher beliefs and stress. *Journal of Rational Emotive and Cognitive Behavior Therapy*, 34, 209–224.

Berryhill, J., Linney, J. A., & Fromewick, J. (2009). The effects of education accountability on teachers: Are policies too stress provoking for their own good? *International Journal of Education Policy and Leadership*, 4, 1–14.

Borg, M. G., Riding, R. J., & Falzon, J. M. (1991). Stress in teaching: A study of occupational stress and its determinants, job satisfaction and career commitment among primary school teachers. *Educational Psychology*, 11, 59–75.

Brown, M. & Ralph, S. (1992). Towards the identification of stress in teachers. *Educational Research*, 48, 103–110.

Cappella, E., Frazier, S. L., Atkins, M. S., Schoenwald, S. K., & Glisson, C. (2008). Enhancing schools' capacity to support children in poverty: An ecological model of school-based mental health services. *Administration and Policy in Mental Health*, 35, 395–409.

Carver-Thomas, D. & Darling-Hammond, L. (2017). Teacher turnover: Why it matters and what we can do about it. Research Brief for the Learning Policy Institute, September, 2017. Accessed online at https://learningpolicyinstitute.org/sites/default/files/productfiles/Teacher_Turnover_BRIEF.pdf.

Cook-Cottone, C. P. (2015). *Mindfulness and Yoga for Embodied Self-Regulation: A Primer for Mental Health Professionals*. New York, NY: Springer Publishing.

Cox, T., Boot, N., Cox, S., & Harrison, S. (1988). Stress in schools: An organizational perspective. *Work and Stress*, 2, 353–362.

Deloitte Center for Health Solutions. (2017). *At a Tipping Point? Workplace Mental Health and Wellbeing*. London: Author.

Denzin, N. K. (2007). *On Understanding Emotion*. New Brunswick, NJ: Transaction Publishers.

Educator Quality of Work Life Survey. (2017). American Federation of Teachers and BAT's.

Emmons, R. (2010, November 16). Why gratitude is good. Retrieved from: https://greatergood.berkeley.edu/article/item/why_gratitude_is_good.

Fantuzzo, J., Perlman, S., Sproul, F., Minney, A., Perry, M. A., & Li, F. (2012). Making visible teacher reports of their teaching experiences: The early childhood teacher experiences scale. *Psychology in the Schools*, 49(2),194–205.

Figley, C. R. (Ed.). (1995). *Brunner/Mazel Psychological Stress Series, No. 23. Compassion Fatigue: Coping with Secondary Traumatic Stress Disorder in Those Who Treat the Traumatized*. Philadelphia, PA: Brunner/Mazel.

Frenzel, A. C., Goetz, T., Ludtke, O., Pekrun, R., & Sutton, R. (2009). Emotional transmission in the classroom: Exploring the relationship between teacher and student enjoyment. *Journal of Educational Psychology*, 101(3), 705–716.

Green, J. G., McLaughlin, K. A., Alegría, M., Costello, E. J., Gruber, M. J., Hoagwood, K., & Kessler, R. C. (2013).

School mental health resources and adolescent mental health service use. *Journal of the American Academy of Child & Adolescent Psychiatry*, 52, 501–510.

Greenberg, M. T., Brown, J. L., & Abenavoli, R. M. (2016). *Teachers' Stress and Health Effects on Teachers, Students, and Schools*. Edna Bennett Pierce Prevention Research Center, Pennsylvania State University. Issue Brief.

Guglielmi, R. S. & Tatrow, K. (1998). Occupational stress, burnout, and health in teachers: A methodological and theoretical analysis. *Review of Educational Research*, 68, 61–99.

Halifax, J. (2018). *Standing at the Edge: Finding Freedom Where Fear and Courage Meet*. New York, NY: Flatiron Books.

Hall, E., Woodhouse, D. A., & Wooster, A. D. (1986). Reducing teacher stress. *British Journal of InService Educational Evaluation and Policy Analysis*, 14, 72–74, 80.

Hargreaves, A. (2001). Emotional geographies of teaching. *Teachers College Record*, 103(6), 1056–1080.

Harris, A. R., Jennings, P. A., Katz, D. A., Abenavoli, R. M., & Greenberg, M. T. (2015, November 4). Promoting stress management and wellbeing in educators: Feasibility and efficacy of a school-based yoga and mindfulness intervention. *Mindfulness*. DOI 10.1007/s12671-015-0451-2.

Hattie, J. & Yates, G. (2014). *Visible Learning and the Science of How We Learn*. New York, NY: Routledge.

Hellebuyck, M., Nguyen, T., Halphern, M., Fritze, D., & Kennedy, J. (2017). *Mind the Workplace: A Brief from Mental Health America*. Alexandria, VA: Mental Health America.

Hochschild, A. R. (1983). *The Managed Heart: Commercialization of Human Feeling*. Berkeley, CA: University of California Press.

Hughes, R. E. (2001). Deciding to leave but staying: Teacher burnout, precursors and turnover. *The International Journal of Human Resource Management*, 12(2), 288–298.

Ingersoll, R. M. (2004). Why do high-poverty schools have difficulty staffing their classrooms with qualified teachers?

A Joint Initiative of the Center for American Progress and the Institute for America's Future.

Isenbarger, L. & Zembylas, M. (2006). The emotional labour of caring in teaching. *Teaching and Teacher Education, 22,* 120–134.

Jennings, P. A., Brown, J. L., Frank, J. L., Doyle, S., Oh, Y., Davis, R., Rasheed, D., DeWeese, A., DeMauro, A. A., Cham, H., & Greenberg, M. T. (2017). February 13. Impacts of the CARE for teachers program on teachers' social and emotional competence and classroom interactions. *Journal of Educational Psychology.* Advance online publication. DOI http://dx.doi.org/10.1037/edu0000187.

Jennings, P. A. & Greenberg, M. T. (2009). The prosocial classroom: Teacher social and emotional competence in relation to student and classroom outcomes. *Review of Educational Research,* 79(1), 491–525.

Kabat-Zinn, J. (1990). *Full Catastrophe Living: Using the Wisdom of Your Body and Mind to Face Stress, Pain, and Illness.* New York, NY: Bantam Dell.

Kabat-Zinn, J. (1994). *Wherever You Go, There You Are: Mindfulness Meditation in Everyday Life.* New York, NY: Hyperion.

Kemeny, M. E., Foltz, C., Cavanaugh, J. F., Cullen, M., Giese-Davis, J., Jennings, P. A., & Ekman, P. (2012). Contemplative/emotion training reduces negative emotional behavior and promotes prosocial responses. *Emotion, 12,* 338–350.

Kim, K. (2018). *Mindful Practices Social Emotional Learning Framework Teacher Competency for SY2017-18.* Retrieved from Chicago.

Klusmann, U, Kunter, M., Trautwein, U., Ludtke, O., & Baumert, J. (2008). Teachers' occupational well-being and quality of instruction: The important role of self-regulatory patterns. *Journal of Educational Psychology,* 100(3), 702–715.

Kovess-Masféty, V., Rios-Seidel, C., & Sevilla-Dedieu, C. (2007). Teachers' mental health and teaching levels. *Teaching and Teacher Education, 23,* 1177–1192.

Lam, B.-h. (2019). Social support giving and teacher development. In *Social Support, Well-Being, and Teacher Development* (pp. 241–277). Singapore: Springer Singapore.

Laughlin, A. (1984). Teacher stress in an Australian setting: The role of biographical mediators. *Educational Studies*, 10, 7–22.

Lomas, T., Medina, J. C., Ivtzan, I., Rupprecht, S., & Eiroa-Orosa, F. J. (2017). The impact of mindfulness on the wellbeing and performance of educators: A systematic review of the empirical literature. *Teaching and Teacher Education*, 61, 132–141.

McLean, L. & Connor, C. M. (2015). Depressive symptoms in third grade teachers: Relations to classroom quality and student achievement. *Child Development*, 86, 945–954.

Metlife. (2013). *The Metlife Survey of the American Teacher: Challenges for Leadership*. New York, NY: Author.

Oberle, E. & Schonert-Reichl, K. A. (2016). Stress contagion in the classroom? The link between classroom teacher burnout and morning cortisol in elementary school students. *Social Science and Medicine*, 159, 30–37.

Oplatka, I. (2009). Emotion management and display in teaching: Some ethical and moral considerations in the era of marketization and commercialization. In P. A. Shutz & M. Zembylas (Eds.), *Advances in Teacher Emotion Research: The Impact on Teachers' Lives* (pp. 55–71). New York, NY: Springer.

Ouellette, R. R., Frazier, S. L., Shernoff, E. S., Cappella, E., Mehta, T. G., Maríñez-Lora, A., … Atkins, M. S. (2018). Teacher job stress and satisfaction in urban schools: Disentangling individual-, classroom-, and organizational-level influences. *Behavior Therapy*, 49(4),494–508.

Pekrun, R., Frenzel, A. C., Goetz, T., & Perry, R. P. (2007). The control-value theory of achievement emotions: An integrative approach to emotions in education. In P. A. Shutz & R. Pekrun (Eds.), *Emotion in Education* (pp. 13–36). Amsterdam: Academic Press.

Pierce, M. B. & Molloy, G. N. (1990). Psychological and biographical differences between secondary school teachers experiencing high and low levels of burnout. *British Journal of Educational Psychology*, 60, 37–51.

Punch, K. F. & Tuettemann, E. (1990). Correlates of psychological distress among secondary school teachers. *British Educational Research Journal*, 16, 369–382.

Roeser, R. W. (2014). The emergence of mindfulness-based interventions in educational settings. *Motivational Interventions: Advances in Motivation and Achievement*, 18, 379–419.

Rogers, J. (October, 2017). Teaching and learning in the age of Trump: Increasing stress and hostility in America's high schools. *A Report Issued by UCLA's Institute for Democracy, Education, and Access*.

Rones, M. & Hoagwood, K. (2000). School-based mental health services: A research review. *Clinical Child and Family Psychology Review*, 3, 223–241.

Ronfeldt, M., Lankford, H., Loeb, S., & Wyckoff, J. (2013). How teacher turnover harms student achievement. *American Educational Research Journal*, 50, 4–36.

Saakvitne, K. W., & Pearlman, L. A. (1996). *Transforming the Pain: A Workbook on Vicarious Traumatization*. New York, NY: W. W. Norton & Company.

Schwarzer, R. & Hallum, S. (2008). Perceived teacher self-efficacy as a predictor of job stress and burnout: Mediation analysis. *Applied Psychology*, 57, 152–171.

Shernoff, E. S., Mehta, T. G., Atkins, M. S., Torf, R., & Spencer, J. (2011). A qualitative study of the sources and impact of stress among urban teachers. *School Mental Health*, 3(2), 59–69.

Van der Kolk, B. A. (2014). *The Body Keeps the Score: Brain, Mind, and Body in the Healing of Trauma*. New York, NY: Viking.

Vozza, S. (2017). Why employees at Apple and Google are more productive. *Fast Company*. March 13, 2017. Accessed online at www.fastcompany.com/3068771/howemployees-at-apple-and-google-are-more-productive.

Yang, X., Ge, C., Hu, B., Chi, T., & Wang, L. (2009). Relationship between quality of life and occupational stress among teachers. *Public Health*, 123(11), 750–755.

Zhou, J. (2012). The effects of reciprocal imitation on teacher-student relationships and student learning outcomes. *Mind, Brain, and Education*, 6(2), 66–73.

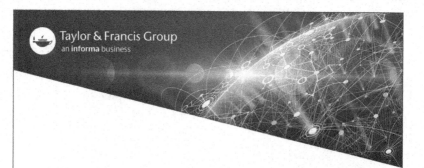